JUSTIN SMITH MORRILL

Justin Smith Morrill of Strafford, Vermont. Courtesy of the Vermont Division for Historic Preservation, Montpelier, Vermont.

JUSTIN SMITH MORRILL

Father of the Land-Grant Colleges

Coy F. Cross II

Michigan State University Press
East Lansing

∞ The paper used in this publication meets the minimum require-
ments of ANSI/NISO Z39.48–1992 (R 1997) (Permanence of
Paper).

Michigan State University Press
East Lansing, Michigan 48823-5202

04 03 02 01 00 99   1 2 3 4 5 6 7 8 9

Library of Congress Cataloging-in-Publication Data

Cross, Coy F.
  Justin Smith Morrill : father of the land-grant colleges / Coy F.
Cross II.
    p. cm.
  Includes bibliographical references (p.) and index.

  ISBN 0-87013-508-2 (alk. paper)
  1. Morrill, Justin S. (Justin Smith), 1810-1898. 2. United
States. Congress. Senate--Biography. 3. Legislators--United
States--Biography. 4. State universities and colleges--United
States--History. I. Title.
  E664.M8 C76 1999
  973.6'6'092--dc21
  [B]
                                99-6502
                                CIP

Cover design by Heidi Dailey.
Book design by Michael J. Brooks

Visit Michigan State University Press on the World-Wide Web at:
www.msu.edu/unit/msupress

Dedicated to all Vermonters, everywhere,
especially those in Strafford

CONTENTS

FOREWORD

Justin Smith Morrill, more than any public figure in the nineteenth century, changed higher education in America. Born in Strafford, Vermont, in 1810, Morrill rose above his modest beginnings to become a wealthy and highly successful entrepreneur. His business ventures were so successful, in fact, that he retired at the age of thirty-eight to become a farmer and eventually to enter into the turbulent world of mid-nineteenth-century politics. On the eve of the American Civil War, in 1854, he was elected to the U.S. House of Representatives from Vermont. For the next forty-three years he served in Congress, first as a member of the House, then as a member of the Senate after 1867.

He is best remembered for his work that transformed American higher education. Morrill had a vision of education that was articulated in part by Thomas Jefferson; both believed that the future success of American democracy rested on the nation's ability to maintain an informed and educated electorate. But, whereas Jefferson's version of that philosophy took root gradually at his beloved University of Virginia, Justin Smith Morrill, the practical, small-town Yankee entrepreneur, galvanized this "radical" notion by crafting an elegant, practical mechanism that insured success on a grand scale.

In the dark days of 1862, when the Union's armies seemed to be losing the war on every front, Representative Morrill pressed his case for higher education's future with skeptical and more short-sighted congressional colleagues. Looking beyond the Civil War's day-to-day crises, he understood that existing colleges and universities could not possibly meet the future educational needs of America's burgeoning population. To be sure, there were academies to train teachers; universities existed to educate members of the clergy, to train physicians, and to teach "the classics." There were, however, only a few schools where the "agricultural and industrial classes," as he called them, could receive the education they so badly needed. On 2 July 1862, Morrill prevailed and, one day after another Union military defeat, this one at the Battle of Malvern Hill, President Abraham Lincoln signed into law the Land-Grant Act of 1862, or as it is known today, the First Morrill Act.

The First Morrill Act and a series of related laws, including the Hatch Act of 1887, the Second Morrill Act of 1890, and the Smith-Lever Act of 1914, established the system of Land-Grant colleges and universities throughout the United States. Specifically, they set aside what were called "endowment lands" to generate revenue to fund the Land-Grant schools and to subsidize the teaching of courses in the "agricultural and industrial arts." Legislatures in Michigan, Pennsylvania, and Iowa were the first to respond to Morrill's new law; each restructured one of their newly established colleges in accordance with provisions of the Land-Grant Act. These schools would become America's first Land-Grant institutions: Michigan State University, Pennsylvania State University, and Iowa State University.

Since 1862, more than 20 million Americans, men and women of every race, ethnicity, religion, and economic background have been educated by Land-Grant colleges and universities. Agricultural experiment stations and cooperative extension offices have transformed agrarian life and American agriculture. Innovations spawned at Land-Grant schools have revolutionized our scientific, technological, and physical landscapes. Notwithstanding these contributions, Land-Grant schools also provide an outstanding education for those seeking careers in medicine, law, and government, as well as in the liberal arts and humanities.

Teaching, research, and public service always have been hallmarks at Land-Grant universities. In recent decades, many institutions of higher learning have adopted these basic Land-Grant school concepts to varying degrees to the benefit of all. Land-Grant schools continue to play a special and distinctive role in America. In one way or another, work by Land-Grant scholars and researchers has affected, and will continue to affect, every person living in the United States.

It has been seventy-five years since William Belmont Parker published *The Life and Public Services of Justin Smith Morrill*; it has been out of print for some time. This long overdue, new biography provides a refreshing, up-to-date view of Morrill's life and his contributions to American politics and higher education. Coy Cross has gone back to the primary sources, reviewing the Morrill correspondence and the many official documents and papers generated during the senator's long and illustrious career. Cross, in his final analysis, has shown us how one Vermont businessman-turned-politician helped to shape the modern world.

Peter McPherson
President
Michigan State University

PREFACE

Justin Smith Morrill served in Congress from 1855 until his death in 1898, longer than anyone had ever served before. As a member and chair of the House Ways and Means and the Senate Finance Committees, he, more than any other individual, shaped tax and tariff legislation throughout his long tenure. His most lasting contributions, however, were his 1862 and 1890 bills creating and supporting land-grant colleges. The 1862 bill was perhaps the greatest education legislation in American history. Designed to provide a practical education for working people, the 1862 bill expanded curricula to include all branches of engineering, agricultural sciences, veterinary medicine, and the vast majority of other subjects we study today. The measure also made college accessible to working classes, women, African-Americans, immigrants, and other minorities. Over 20 million people have graduated from the more than 100 land-grant institutions.

Yet, sadly, few of today's college students, even at the land-grant institutions, know who opened the door to higher education for them. William B. Parker's *The Life and Public Service of Justin Smith Morrill* (Boston: Houghton Mifflin Company, 1924), the only published biography, has long been out of print. Morrill seems everywhere forgotten, except in his home state of Vermont and especially in Strafford, his hometown. In 1997 Education Television of Vermont produced *Land for Learning: Justin Morrill and America's Land-Grant Colleges and Universities* and made it available to Public Broadcasting System stations nationwide. In July 1998 the citizens of Strafford, with the help of the University of Vermont, Michigan State University, Pennsylvania State

University, and the National Association of State Universities and Land-Grant Colleges, sponsored a two-day seminar entitled *Land for Learning*, on Morrill and his legacy. Hopefully, the video, the symposium and this biography will help refresh the memory of those who have forgotten Morrill's contributions and enlighten those who were never aware.

I must express a special "Thank You!" to Gwenda Smith, Strafford historian, John Dumville, Vermont Office of Historic Preservation, John Freitag, President of the Strafford Historical Society, all the volunteers at the Morrill Homestead, and the citizens of Strafford, Vermont, whose help and encouragement made the work possible. Also, I want to thank David English and the staff at the Beale Air Force Base Library for their efforts in locating and obtaining important documents. The staffs at the Library of Congress, Cornell University's Carl A. Kroch Library, Dartmouth College's Baker Library, Duke University Library, Harvard University Library, Syracuse University Library, University of Vermont's Bailey/Howe Library, and the Vermont and Massachusetts Historical Societies. I also owe my wife Carol a special thanks for her unfailing faith and support.

THE MAKING OF JUSTIN MORRILL

Anyone can be a Vermonter—anyone who subscribes to a doctrine of frugality, self-reliance, and humility, who takes up residence in the hills and pays his poll tax—but to be a good Vermonter, native or immigrant, he has to have an eccentricity; somewhere in his background there is a gentle madness, a persistent fanaticism, an honest idiosyncrasy.[1]

Justin Smith Morrill was both typical and atypical of Vermont's citizens in the nineteenth century. He was a Vermont blacksmith's son, but his tastes were those of the English gentry. He could not afford college, but through reading and studying he became a well-educated man and earned several honorary degrees. He opposed women's suffrage, the eight-hour workday, and direct election of the president and senators, but he supported college education for the masses, including women and blacks. His career began as a store clerk, but he retired a relatively wealthy man at age 38. Then, after retirement, he began a political career that lasted forty-three years. Clearly, he was a complex man, who did not fit into a rigidly defined niche.

Although Morrill had a house in Washington, his home and his roots were in Vermont. And those roots were deep. Abraham Morrill, Justin's great, great, great-grandfather, arrived at Cambridge, Massachusetts, from England in 1632, just 12 years after the *Mayflower* landed at Plymouth. By 1780, when Justin's father Nathaniel was born, the family had moved a short distance to Chichester, New Hampshire. In 1795 Grandfather Smith Morrill, his wife Mary, five sons and two daughters joined the migration stimulated by Vermont's admission to statehood four years earlier.

One historian defined those migrating to Vermont as settlers seeking to establish "self-sustaining homes in a congenial environment." They were neither fleeing religious persecution, coming as conquerors, nor acting as agents for a large company. "They wanted only the freedom of a virgin land."[2] The new state was still largely wilderness with barely 85,000 people. The immigrants would help shape Vermont, but Vermont would help mold them, too. As historian Lee Storrs said, "The hardy farm life, rock-strewn hillsides, the rough winters and rough roads, the tense conservatism, the domination of the one-room school and the village church, all had something to do with the character-making of the men of the mountains."[3] Justin Morrill described Strafford's early settlers as "possessing a large share of brain power, plenty of muscle, and they lived long, unfolding wit and wisdom and much originality of character."[4]

Strafford must have attracted the Morrill family. Smith, Mary and their family stopped in South Strafford (Lower Village then), on the West Branch of the Ompompanoosuc River. Sons David and Daniel stayed there, while Nathaniel, Stephen, Joseph, and their parents and sisters moved two and one-half miles farther to Strafford (Upper Village then) a short time later. Smith and his sons soon had a thriving blacksmith business with shops in both the villages. Using the mountain stream for power, the Morrills added trip-hammers to both shops and made axes, hoes and scythes for the local farmers.[5]

The Morrills prospered in Strafford and, in 1806, Nathaniel married Mary Hunt, "a woman of superior character and education."[6] A neighbor described Mary as an admirable woman with above average intelligence and culture. He also commented on her "ladylike manners" and "excellent wifely and motherly qualities." She was, according to the neighbor, "an excellent female citizen." One of her sons remembered her good humor and calm disposition. He also recalled her kindness, an attribute he believed his brother Justin had inherited.[7]

Nathaniel and Mary had ten children, but only five lived to adulthood. Caroline B., the oldest, died at 15. Justin later reminisced about her "large and lovely brown eyes and her constant care" for him and dedicated a poem entitled "An imperfect token of remembrance of my dear departed sister."[8] Justin Smith, born 14 April 1810, came next. His mother apparently named him for Justin Smith, a "learned and capable physician." Twins, Sidney Smith and Edna M., arrived five years later. Sidney became a Fulton, New York, jeweler. Edna married Dr. Ephraim Carpenter and moved to Troy, New York. Sidney and Edna lived to be among the oldest twins in the United States. She died at 91 and he at 96. Nathaniel Batchelder, born in 1818, lived only seven years. Amos, born two years later, spent his life in Strafford and carried on the family tradition as the village blacksmith. In 1825, a second Caroline was born, but she lived less than a year. Wilbur Fisk, born in 1826, became a dentist in New Albany, Indiana. The last of Nathaniel and Mary's children were a second set of twins that apparently died at birth and remained unnamed. The early death of so many of their children must have affected Justin's parents and his entire family.[9]

When Justin arrived on 14 April 1810, the United States, barely 21 years old, had 25 states and 7,239,881 people. James Madison was president. George Washington had been dead for eleven years. Abraham Lincoln, who would sign Morrill's Land-Grant College Act, was still in his cradle. Franklin Pierce, who was president when Morrill went to Congress, was six. William McKinley, the last president Morrill served under, would not be born for another 33 years. Vermont had 217,000 people. Jonas Galusha was governor, and Montpelier had been the state capital for only two years.[10] Strafford, a small village surrounded by rolling hills and small farms, consisted of the blacksmith shop, two stores, a tavern, a lawyer's office, a doctor's office, a meeting house and about twenty homes. In a poem, Justin described his "Native Village" as a lovely spot with a steepled church, green hills, a pond and a mill. He loved Strafford where "even the stars, the planets, and the moon seem to shine more brightly than elsewhere."[11] On returning from Europe in 1867, he expressed his thanks to God for permitting him to be born in America, "and in New England rather than in any other part, and in Vermont rather than even in any other State in New England."[12]

In 1814, when Justin was but four, his father and three uncles joined Captain Jedediah H. Harris' light infantry company at Burlington, Vermont, ready to defend Plattsburgh, New York, against the British army. Grandfather Smith Morrill, though sixty-five and lame, also traveled to Burlington to fight the British. When told he could tend the horses, but could not join the battle, Smith cried from disappointment. Captain Harris' company soon learned that other volunteers had already repelled the invaders. Still seeking their moment of glory, Strafford's heroes joined the pursuit of the fleeing British. As a reward for his bravery, Nathaniel became a regimental commander in the state militia. His friends dubbed him "Colonel Nat," a title he wore proudly for the rest of his life. Justin considered his father "the most truly honest man I ever knew."[13] The son always strove to warrant the same praise-worthy epithet.

Justin grew up in a two-storied, white house with green-shuttered windows that reflected his father's status and success. As an adult he fondly remembered the family kitchen with a ceiling so low he had to stoop to avoid drying clothes or dried apples and pumpkins. Otherwise, "I may as well acknowledge I should get a thwack across my noodle or leave my hat like Absalom suspended among the brambles." The Morrill family home still stands, next to the blacksmith shop, and across the Ompompanoosuc from Strafford's meeting hall.[14]

Like most nineteenth-century New England households, the Morrill home was a busy place, where everyone had his or her chores. One of Justin's duties was churning the milk to make butter, a job he did not relish. His mother insisted that he churn in a cool place in the summer and a warm place in the winter, while he "sometimes wished the venerable wooden churn dashed into a still warmer place." Mary's discipline, he admitted, taught him to stick to a task until he finished. Perhaps, the tenacity with which he pursued goals, such as additional funding for the land-grant colleges, can be trace to his mother's persistence.[15]

When Justin was seven, President James Monroe visited Strafford. Mary dressed her son in a new suit, with many buttons and a wide, ruffled collar. A stiff, bell-topped, red "morocco" hat gave the outfit its crowning touch. The family walked the two and a half miles to South Strafford to see the president. Unfortunately, as they waited for President Monroe, who was a few hours late, rain began to fall. The rain caused the dye in the red hat to run and the pasteboard, which gave the hat its illustrious shape, to collapse. The much anticipated event consisted of a brief glimpse of Monroe in a closed coach and a presidential wave to the rain-soaked, roadside crowd. During the long walk home, other boys ridiculed Justin and the other four or five youngsters with their "cardinal head regalia." Only the presence of adults prevented retaliation. Interestingly, Morrill retained the memory of the ridicule and humiliation into his old age.[16]

Justin's education started early, with his mother "inducing" him to read the Bible. He later recalled that he found some of the Old Testament books "tedious," but the Book of Job and the stories of David and Noah were "so attractive as to demand a second reading and sometimes a third." (One wonders what he found "so attractive" in Job's trials and tribulations.) He began formal classes in what he described as an old, "flat square-roofed schoolhouse." The school's interior was a testimonial to the creativity of generations of boys who had used its walls to practice their carving skills through the long, Vermont winters. The building had a huge fireplace where schoolmasters seasoned their birch switches in the hot ashes. When Justin was ten, the town built a two-story, brick school. Wearing another new suit for his first day in the new building, Justin left home early to play with his friends. Since the term began on the first Monday after Thanksgiving, winter had already come to Vermont and the pond behind the school had frozen over during the night. Justin joined his friends sliding across the ice making long scratch marks with the nails in their new shoes. Unfortunately, the ice had a weak spot and Justin broke through, soaking himself and ruining his new suit. Forced to return home for dry clothes, Justin had to endure his mother's scolding then dress in old clothes to begin school. For him, the pond had forever lost its charm.[17]

After finishing his elementary education at Strafford's brick school house, Justin attended the academy ten miles away at Thetford for a three-month term. He then completed another three-month term at Randolph Academy. The academies were similar to today's high schools, but were usually reserved for well-to-do families. Thus, ended Justin Morrill's formal education.[18]

His love for learning, however, prompted him to continue reading and studying throughout his life. While still in elementary school, Justin learned grammar from Daniel Cobb, Strafford's lawyer. Cobb had the boy parse[19] Alexander Pope's *Essay on Man*. Judge Harris, the former militia captain, gave Justin access to his personal library. The boy borrowed the *History of England*, Thomas Jefferson's *Notes on Virginia*, the *Federalist*, and various Sir Walter Scott and James Fenimore Cooper novels.[20]

Although he attended writing and bookkeeping classes while living in Portland, Maine, mostly he was self-taught. "My Sabbath days were early and late devoted either to study or general reading." When he began earning enough to afford them, he bought his own books. Eventually Morrill possessed an impressive library ranging from classic English literature to books on architecture and gardening. These books were not to impress company, they were well-read. In later years Morrill would comment, "It has taken a long time and much labor to obtain whatever has been of any real value to me in the way of a moderate education."[21]

While attending Randolph Academy, Justin had wanted to go to college. But when he asked his father, Nathaniel replied, "I can afford to send you, but I do not know as I could the other boys—Think it over and see what you think best."[22] When Justin mentioned the conversation to Judge Harris, the judge reminded the boy he could pay his own way through college by teaching school during the winter. Judge Harris suggested, however, Justin might be more successful as a merchant, a calling Harris himself had pursued. When Justin finished his term at Randolph Academy, the Tyler-Robinson School District, one of several districts that ran one-room schools in Strafford, offered him a teaching position at $11 per month and room-and-board. But he followed Judge Harris' advice and accepted a clerkship in Royal Hatch's Strafford store, which only provide board.[23] Many years later, however, he told a group of students, "I know it was a great disadvantage to me that I could not go to school."[24] His own inability to attend college probably motivated his support for land-grant colleges and expanded educational opportunity.

After six months with Hatch, sixteen-year-old Justin moved to Judge Harris' store, where he received $45 for the first year and $75 for the second. Morrill remembered the judge spoke with "great force, clearness and pungent wit." He was also a delightful conversationalist, "full of repartee and abounding in a large fund of anecdote." Harris also had a remarkable memory, especially for political history. Morrill considered him "the intellectual peer of the foremost men of the state."[25] Morrill's employment at Harris' store began a close personal-business relationship that shaped the rest of Justin Morrill's life. From this point until his own death, Harris was a primary influence in shaping Justin's life.

Jedediah Hyde Harris, the man who became Justin Morrill's mentor, role model, and second father, was born December 1784 in Norwich, Connecticut. He moved to Strafford before he was 21 years old and opened a store, which was immediately successful. Although limited to an elementary school education, Harris was an avid reader. He educated himself, especially on politics, finance and farming. James Barrett, a Vermont Supreme Court Justice who knew Harris personally, regarded him "as the most clear headed and the most intelligent man in town, as well as one of the most so in the county," and "the peer of the best in the State."[26] His "fine presence" and intellectual ability quickly won the respect of his neighbors, who elected him to the state legislature in 1810, 1812, 1814, and 1818. Harris was a member of the Constitutional Convention of 1814, a county court judge in 1821–22, a member of the

Council of Censors in 1827, a state councilor in 1828–30, and a presidential elector in 1845. He retained the title "judge" for the remainder of his life. Judge Harris spent the last 30 years of his life farming, "of which he was passionately fond and wherein he particularly excelled."[27]

Harris married Judith Young, the daughter of Strafford's first resident minister. Mrs. Harris was a gracious host and a "veritable mother in Grace to the poor and to the afflicted."[28] Many friends and acquaintances enjoyed the Harrises' hospitality. Morrill, a frequent guest himself, compared the Harris home to a "well-patronized hotel," where the guests were always "greeted with good cheer." The Harrises had two daughters, Marcia Ann, born the same year as Justin, and Ellen Janette, two years younger. The girls were Justin's school mates at the village school and at Thetford and Randolph Academies. The young ladies then attended the Ladies' School in Windsor, Vermont, and Mrs. Willard's Seminary in Troy, New York. The "Harris girls," known for their beauty and intellectual brilliance, were the belles of the state and lifelong friends of Justin Morrill. After his seventy-second birthday, he acknowledged Ellen Janette's birthday present with a note thanking her for the gift and for teaching "an awkward boy" to dance at 16.[29]

Besides learning all he could as Judge Harris' clerk, Justin continued reading everything he could find. He even helped start a library association with members paying $2 each. The dues bought books, which all the members shared. After Morrill moved to Portland, Maine, the association dissolved and the remaining books disappeared. A teenaged Justin also participated in the local debating society.[30]

In 1828, with his mother's blessing, "One Spanish Mill Dollar (1787)" (which he still had when he died seventy years later) from his father, and letters of recommendation from Judge Harris, Lawyer Daniel Cobb and Dr. Albigence Pierce, 18-year-old Justin Morrill left Strafford to seek his fortune in Portland, Maine. Dr. Jacob Hunt, his mother's brother, lived in Portland. Uncle Jacob introduced Justin to Daniel Fox, a merchant who shipped lumber to the West Indies and returned with sugar and molasses. Fox immediately hired Morrill as his bookkeeper. Judge Harris obviously had taught his pupil well. A short time later Dr. Hunt advised Justin to accept a clerk's position in Jeremiah Dow's wholesale-retail dry goods store. Morrill worked for Dow for the next two years.[31]

Since Dow's store was not open evenings, Justin had time to continue his self-education. Mr. Codman, a nearby attorney, lent him books, including *Blackstone's Commentaries*. Dr. Hunt, who enjoyed philosophy and English literature, made his personal library available to his nephew. The poet in Justin especially loved the "immortal words" of Lord Byron. He also borrowed books from the Portland Library. He polished his writing skills in anonymous articles for the local newspaper, a practice that he had begun in Strafford. One letter to the Portland *Advocate*, for example, criticized the Maine legislators for making it illegal to sell alcohol in less than pint quantities. Signing his article Yankee X, Morrill reasoned, "If people will have rum let them have little as they will." Morrill recalled, "It was glory enough for a mere tyro to see his papers in print and sometimes to hear them read aloud by those who were wholly ignorant of the authorship."[32]

Much of Morrill's social and intellectual activity in Portland centered on "The Club," an organization for "improvement rather than amusement." Young friends gathered to discuss ideas and hear lectures. One evening Morrill and his peers pondered whether the Greeks might have descended from the "Hindoos." Another time the Reverend Doctor Nichols used "first-rate remarks and scientific facts" to prove that good mathematicians did not participate in games of chance.[33]

The long evenings also left time to ponder religion. Even though eastern Vermont had witnessed such intense evangelical "fire" in the mid-1830s that areas became known as "burned-over districts," Morrill rejected the doctrine that people were innately bad and would burn in Hell without a conversion experience. Instead, he preferred the more rational, nonevangelical Universalist teachings. Universalists believed God rewarded or punished people during their lifetime, according to their deeds, but afforded salvation to everyone.[34] Morrill would later switch to Unitarianism.

Justin's diary from Portland reveals different sides of his personality. The young man tended toward arrogance calling his customers "backwoods" or "starched up gentry," (to his diary, not to their faces). The "pungent wit" Morrill attributed to Judge Harris was also apparent in his protege. "Friendship," he wrote, "does not choke with fun, although it should *cut* now and then." Young Morrill admitted he did not often "approach the shrine of wit," but when he did "folks should be ready to laugh tho' they could cry out '*murther* (mother)!'"[35] The mature Morrill would avoid both the arrogance and the sarcastic humor.

The diary also provides insight into Justin Morrill's attitudes toward and appreciation for women. Although six-feet tall, handsome, with dark wavy hair, and clear blue eyes, he was still ill-at-ease in direct conversations with women. "So it is ever when one wishes to be masterly agreeable the spirit-of-talk ever forsakes him." Yet, he could be poetic from afar. A young woman, whom he only saw in a second-story window, had "the finest proportions and easy grace, with a complexion made almost bewitching by the glow of candle-light, of maiden beauty that I ever recollect seeing displayed." Young Justin, however, did not approve of women wearing "pantalets," "a goose with britches on would be a far more lovely sight!" Also, he dubbed a woman customer, who aggressively asserted her point, "one of these female wise-acres." As Morrill matured he became more comfortable around women and maintained lifelong friendships with several. Yet, Senator Morrill did not support women's suffrage. Perhaps he still believed as he did at 20 years old "the major part of the dear ones prefer mirth to knowledge."[36]

A few months later, in the autumn of 1830, Morrill returned to Strafford to visit his family. While he was there, Colonel Ralph Hosford, a merchant in South Strafford, died suddenly. His partners sought someone to sell the stock on hand and close the business. Judge Harris recommended Justin and the partners offered him the position. After obtaining his release from his employer in Portland, he accepted. The following spring, after Morrill had completed his task at Hosford's store, Judge Harris proposed forming a partnership under the name Harris and Morrill. Harris would capitalize the venture with $2,500, which the firm would repay, plus 6 per cent annual interest. The partners would share equally in all business profits.[37]

By the spring of 1831, Morrill had five years experience in the retail business, two under the tutelage of Judge Harris. He also knew double-entry bookkeeping. So Judge Harris left his junior partner to run the store while he retired to his first love, farming. Like Harris, Morrill sold merchandise on credit and insisted that all customers settle accounts by January 1. If the debtor could not settle in full, the unpaid balance became a six-percent note, secured by property if possible.[38]

The partners paid cash for their merchandise, assuring themselves the best purchase prices. Morrill traveled to Boston in April and September to purchase stock for the summer and winter months. He returned with five to six tons of goods on a large freight wagon drawn by four or six horses. The business grew until the partners had four stores, one in Strafford, one in South Strafford, another in a nearby village, and one in Derby Line, eighty miles away. For a while, Morrill personally ran the South Strafford store. Morrill biographer William Parker described the young grocer as urbane and "unyieldingly" firm, but never known to "show anger or enmity toward any person."[39]

In the nineteenth-century, the general store was a combination department store, furniture store, grocery, and meat market. It also served as the post office, meeting hall, and political and social club. Townspeople and local farmers bought, sold, and bartered around the heating stove. The village sages swapped the latest gossip and news. In Vermont, where everyone took their civil duties seriously, politics was the favorite topic at the general store. Morrill and his friends and neighbors undoubtedly had heated exchanges over Texas' annexation, the Mexican War, and the causes of the 1837 depression. Slavery, which they universally condemned, must also have been a favorite topic. Those who frequented his store quickly learned to respect his opinions and often sought his advice.[40]

In 1839 Morrill apparently considered leaving the general store to become a traveling salesman and collector for a firm in Plymouth. Judge Harris was reluctant to see him go and must have convinced him to stay. Instead of moving, Morrill formed a new partnership with Harris and N. S. Young, in the spring of 1840, under the name Morrill, Young and Company. With the change, Morrill took over Judge Harris' old store in Strafford, where Justin had worked as a boy. He continued there until he retired a few years later.[41]

Yet Morrill and Judge Harris' partnership entailed much more than store ownership. Harris had invested wisely and widely. He owned stock in banks, railroads, and manufacturing. He also owned considerable real estate. The Judge made much of his fortune, however, in lending money and buying and selling personal secured-notes. These business secrets the mentor passed on to his pupil. Morrill was a fast learner. He, too, bought stock in banks, in railroads, and in manufacturing. He invested in real estate. And, he lent money and bought and sold personal secured-notes. Eventually, the teacher often relied on the student's judgment on investments. As a testament to the partners' business acumen, their businesses prospered throughout the terrible depression that lasted from 1837 to 1843.[42]

Morrill also learned to handle his money wisely. He invested most of his money and kept very little ready cash. Family and friends could borrow without paying interest, but Morrill expected them to repay the loan at the agreed time. Sol Carpenter, possibly a relative of sister Edna, borrowed $40 but did not pay when he had committed to. After Carpenter failed to respond to Morrill letters asking for payment, Morrill went to Carpenter's boss in the Interior Department to get the money. Neither Harris nor Morrill forgave loans if there was a possibility of collecting.[43]

In 1841 Morrill took a trip west to collect outstanding partnership debts. He combined business with pleasure and journeyed to Illinois, traveling through New York, Washington, D.C., Virginia, Kentucky, Ohio, Indiana, and Michigan along the way. He thoroughly enjoyed his trip. While visiting his cousin in Illinois, he spent a day bird hunting. He killed "quails, mourning doves, red-winged black birds, plovers, etc." He bragged, "I may say that to-day . . . I have not missed whether on the wing or at rest."[44]

His daily journal also reflected his admiration for the pretty women he encountered. A young Quaker woman attracted his notice, but he "only attracted the notice of her mother at her side." In Cleveland, Ohio, he met a young lady with "large swimming eyes!—who was disposed to flirt." But at Saratoga, New York, he saw the "idol of [his] eyes," "the perfect woman . . . [with] grace in every step, heaven in her eye." He "could have loved her and asked no questions."[45]

Morrill's journal discloses other attitudes and values, including his bias against Africans and African-Americans. While sailing down the Hudson, he shared passage with the "*Amistad* captives."[46] Although the African celebrities charmed most passengers, he considered them the "coarsest samples of Blacks." Later, in Louisville, Kentucky, he admitted to being so "squeamish" about slaves preparing food that he had no appetite. Then, while riding through the Kentucky countryside, he encountered a toll agent beating a slave. Morrill suggested the agent report the slave to his master, instead of beating him. Morrill congratulated himself on doing more for the "amelioration of the condition of the slave" than any abolitionist he knew. "I saved this darkee from further beating," he wrote with obvious self-satisfaction. His attitude would be clearly racist by today's standards. But Morrill's views were similar to those held by nearly all antislavery men of his day, including Abraham Lincoln: blacks were equal legally, but not socially.[47]

Morrill's account of his time in Washington, however, revealed most about his interests and foreshadowed his future. He was quite pleased when someone in Baltimore mistook him for a member of Congress. When he visited his own congressman, however, Morrill found him to be a "miserable wreck," destroyed by "thirst for office and the 'rosy god of wine.'" Watching the proceedings in the House of Representatives decreased his "confidence in men" and made him more "tenacious about measures." Pondering the chances of success in politics, Morrill compared political ambition to "chasing a bauble," since few elected to Congress gain eminence. Obviously, for him, an office without eminence was not worth having.[48]

The city and the Capitol impressed him. He considered a view of the buildings to be worth a trip from the farthest parts of the nation. The style and beauty of the Capitol especially caught his eye. He believed every American child should study the paintings and sculpture in the rotunda. The Capitol was "worthy of a nation, and as one of the nation" he felt proud of it. As a senator, he would be instrumental in beautifying both the building and the city.[49]

But for the present he returned to Strafford and his business duties. Judge Harris continued to share the business expertise he had gained from 40 years experience. His student learned well. So well that in 1848, at 38 years old, Morrill sold his interest in the stores and, with an accumulated wealth of $25–30,000, retired. Although he became a director of the Orange County Bank, Morrill, like Judge Harris, was ready to spend most of his time farming. The lessons in economics and sound business practices Morrill learned from Judge Harris prepared him well to be a "gentleman farmer."[50]

The year before his "retirement," Justin began work on a home. He acquired fifty acres from Judge Harris on the main road through Strafford. Characteristically, Morrill immersed himself in architectural books until he became expert enough to design the house himself. His library still contains copies of Andrew Jackson Downing's books, including *Cottage Residences*, which includes a "Cottage in the Old English Style." Morrill's home is similar to Downing's cottage. The "English or Rural Gothic" style house, with pointed arches and repeating "stalactite drips," was a radical departure from the village's traditional architecture. The exterior was the color of sandstone. Painters mixed sand with the paint to further emphasize the effect.[51]

The house also reflects Morrill's love of books and learning. Perhaps, the home's most beautiful room is the library, which he added a few years later. Here his favorite books and pictures still line the walls. A large, hand-painted skylight provides the reader with natural light. The most captivating feature, however, is the window. It appears to be stained glass, but, instead, the scenes were hand-painted on the glass with paints are so translucent the sun readily shines through. The upper pane depicts the ruins of Hollyrood Abbey, in Edinborough, Scotland, a sight Morrill visited in 1867. The lower pane pictures an unidentified, and possibly imaginary, scene in England. This must have been Morrill's sanctuary and his favorite room in the house.[52]

Morrill also designed the gardens and grounds. Again, he relied heavily on Downing. Morrill subscribed to "The Horticulturist," a journal edited by Downing, and owned at least two Downing books on gardening. Morrill planned to be an experimental horticulturist, instead of a working farmer. The plans for the gardens reflect the same expertise and attention to detail as the plans for the house. More than 100 varieties of trees and shrubs, many not native to Vermont, would grace the grounds. The aroma and color of forty-nine varieties of roses, seven of peonies, six of gladiolus, twelve of tulips, and nearly thirty other kinds of flowers would beautify the gardens. Eighteen varieties of apples, fifteen of pears, seventeen of currants and gooseberries, also cherries, blackberries, raspberries, strawberries, and other fruits and nuts would please the palate of the gentleman farmer and his guests.[53]

Six free-flowing, arabesque flower beds displayed most of the flowers. Others formed a cornucopia. Opposite the veranda, the fleur-de-lis, reserved for the roses, formed the most beautiful and ornate of the flower beds. The soothing sound of a fountain, with a constantly overflowing basin, added to the charm of the gardens. A strolling path allowed ladies in long skirts to walk among the flowers with ease. An elaborate system of stone aqueducts, fed by a pond high on the hillside, provided water for the gardens and the fountain. The house and adjoining gardens would be a showplace. But it was also a warm home where the Morrills would entertain their families and friends. After Judge Harris died, the Morrill home became Strafford's social center. Although Morrill eventually built a house in Washington, the Strafford house was always his home.[54]

In 1848 Justin Morrill must have ranked high on Vermont's "most eligible bachelor" list. As a bright, handsome, successful, thirty-eight year old, who recited and wrote poetry, he surely caught the interest of the belles of New England. His cousin Jedediah N. Morrill and his friend B. F. "Frank" Tenney both tried to play matchmaker for Justin. And, Justin was more than willing to take a bride. Caira Langdon of Montpelier charmed him with her claim to be a "magnetic sorceress." Miss Lucy Ann Fox of Portland was also a potential Mrs. Justin Smith Morrill.[55]

But he had already met Ruth Barrell Swan, a distant relative of the Harris family and a visitor to their home in 1847. The daughter of Dr.

Caleb Swan of Easton, Massachusetts, Ruth was a beautiful, slender, graceful, and charming school teacher. Their romance blossomed as Justin built the house in Strafford. He even traveled to Roxbury, Massachusetts, where Ruth was teaching, for an evening of backgammon and conversation. Eventually, he proposed and Ruth accepted. Biographer William Parker noted, "In this, as in all the major decisions of his life, Morrill had moved with the serene judgment and deliberation that marked his nature."[56] Dr. Swan, a founder of the prohibition movement, approved, even though his future son-in-law did appreciate good wine and occasionally drank whiskey. Justin was 41 and Ruth was 30 when they married in her home on 17 September 1851. The future held great promise for the prosperous country gentleman and his lady as they began their life together in their new home.[57]

The marital bliss was interrupted only two weeks after the wedding, however, when Ruth was "seized by an epileptic fit" while on a train trip to Burlington. Justin attributed the attack to fatigue and assured himself and Ruth that it was an isolated incident. He also disregarded two other minor episodes. Then, in January 1852, Ruth had a seizure too dramatic to ignore. Justin managed to catch her and prevent her from falling, but she became unconscious and chewed her tongue. Her agony as she awakened made his "heart bleed at every pore." Fearing epilepsy as "an unseen dagger" that would "drive [them] from Paradise," Justin wrote Ruth's father about medicine or treatment that might help her. "I would travel bare-footed and in a hair-shirt to the ends of the earth to obtain it," he lamented. For at least the next 25 years, Ruth suffered an episode of "attacks" every four to six weeks. They usually lasted two or three days, with several occurrences each day. Her father sent medicine that reduced the severity of the attacks and prevented convulsions. According to Justin, Ruth found relief in 1875, after seeking help from Dr. Charles Pearson of Lafayette, Indiana.[58]

Despite the epilepsy, Justin and Ruth apparently lead a happy life together. Their correspondence when they were apart reflects a warm, loving relationship. They wanted children and Justin Harris Morrill, named for his father and Judge Harris, was born 27 April 1853. Tragedy struck Paradise again, however, when young Justin died before his second birthday. The loss of their son grieved both Ruth and Justin. She wrote her parents that she would be content to die, if she could just see her child for a moment. After Justin was in Congress, Ruth sent him a flower from their baby's grave. He responded that he loved the flower for its beauty as he had loved their child. He hoped that her visits to the grave site brought "back all the precious memories that cluster around that dearest departed joy."[59]

Two years later, on 8 October 1857, a second son, James Swan, was born. Morrill doted on James and always included a "kiss for Jimmy" in his letters to his wife. Ruth apparently never tried to have more children. She may have feared that she could pass epilepsy on to her children. But, more likely, her pregnancies aggravated the epilepsy making the seizures more frequent and more violent.[60]

Either during Ruth's pregnancy with James or shortly after his birth, her half-sister Louise came to live with the Morrills. Dr. Swan had remarried after Louise's mother died and the third Mrs. Swan treated her stepdaughter badly. Louise became a permanent member of the Morrill household, perhaps to help care for Ruth and Jimmy during Ruth's seizures. The epilepsy apparently was a family secret. If it was a secret, a sister could be trusted far more than a hired nurse. After Justin became a prominent member of Congress and senator, Ruth was a gracious and charming Washington host, but Louise was always at her side.[61]

Two months after little Justin's death in January 1855, Judge Harris also died on March 8. Judge Harris had loved the child who had been named for him and little Justin's death deeply affected him. He told Ruth, "There was something so manly about him that it almost made one feel a degree of reverence for him." Ruth recalled that after saying this Judge Harris "cried like a child."[62]

Judge Harris' death must have been especially hard for Morrill. Justin's father, Nathaniel, had died a few months earlier. So the death of Justin's "second father," so soon after Nathaniel's and baby Justin's, had to be a severe blow. The judge had taught his protege the business philosophy that Morrill had used to build a considerable fortune. Fairness, honesty, good organization, detailed record keeping, timeliness, and thrift were traits that Morrill learned and had practiced in his own business and would use in Congress. Harris had named Morrill as the executor of his estate, a role the student faithfully filled for his mentor.[63]

Judge Harris had given Morrill his profession, his financial success, and had introduced him to Ruth. The elder partner also shared a love of politics with his younger protege. Despite these personal tragedies, Justin Smith Morrill was about to begin his "second career," one that would earn him a place in history.

Notes

1. Lee W. Storrs, *The Green Mountains of Vermont* (New York: Henry Holt and Company, 1965), 17.
2. Ibid., 23.
3. Ibid., 36.
4. William B. Parker, *The Life and Public Services of Justin Smith Morrill* (Boston: Houghton Mifflin Company, 1924), 13.
5. James Barrett, "Early Life of Justin S. Morrill," *The Vermonter*, 2 (November 1896): 61–68, LOC; Jedediah Morrill, "Genealogy of the Morrill family furnished Uncle Justin by Jedediah Morrill, Dorchester Mass. Sept 3d, 1876," Justin S. Morrill Collection, Cornell University; Parker, *Morrill*, 6; N. S. Young, *Washington Post*, 23 January 1889, LOC.
6. Parker, *Morrill*, 3.
7. Ibid., 8–9.
8. Ibid., 22.
9. Morrill, "Genealogy"; Parker, *Morrill*, 7–8.
10. James Barrett, "Justin Smith Morrill," *The Vermonter* (January 1899), LOC.
11. Parker, *Morrill*, 18, 20.
12. Ibid., 1.
13. Barrett, "Early Life," 61–68, LOC; Parker, *Morrill*, 2–5.
14. Parker, *Morrill*, 7.
15. Ibid.
16. Ibid., 22–23.
17. Morrill to W. H. Barnes, 16 May 1871, LOC; Parker, *Morrill*, 20–21.
18. Ibid.
19. Separate each sentence into its parts and explain the grammatical form, function, and interrelation of each part.
20. Morrill to W. H. Barnes, 16 May 1871, LOC.
21. Morrill to James Barrett, January 1886, LOC. The Morrill Memorial Library, built with funds provided in Louise Swan's will, contains most of Morrill's books and serves as the Strafford public library.
22. Louise Swan, personal notes on Morrill, ca 1910, LOC.
23. Morrill to Barrett, January 1886, LOC; Parker, *Morrill*, 25.
24. Parker, *Morrill*, 10.
25. Morrill to Mary Clemma Hudson, n.d., LOC.
26. Barrett, "Early Life," 61–68, LOC.
27. Ibid.; Morrill to Mary Clemma Hudson, n.d., LOC.
28. Morrill to Hudson, n.d., LOC.
29. Ibid.; Parker, *Morrill*, 52.
30. Morrill autobiographical data, n.d., LOC.
31. Ibid.
32. Ibid.; Morrill diary, 18 June 1830, LOC; *Portland Advocate*, 1830, Baker Library, Dartmouth College.
33. Morrill diary, 24 May, 17 and 30 June 1830, LOC.

34. Randolph A. Roth, *The Democratic Dilemma* (Cambridge: Cambridge University Press, 1987), 2, 64–65.

35. Morrill diary, entries 23 and 27 April and 17 May 1830.

36. Ibid., 28 April, 20 and 22 May, and 9 and 30 June 1830.

37. Morrill autobiographical data, n.d., LOC.

38. Morrill to W. H. Barnes; 16 May 71; Young, *Washington Post*.

39. Ibid.; Parker, *Morrill*, 31.

40. Parker, *Morrill*, 31–32.

41. Ibid., 33; Morrill to Isaac Tyson, 12 July 1839, Morrill Collection, Vermont Historical Society.

42. See Judge Harris to Morrill, 4 August 1851 and 26 March 1852, LOC, for example.

43. Morrill to Sol Carpenter, 29 September and 29 December 1879; Morrill to W. B. Thompson, 4 June 1880; Thompson to Morrill, 10 June 1880; W. F. Morrill to Justin Morrill, 2 April 1860; Morrill to Henry C. White, 25 May 1875, LOC.

44. Justin Morrill, "Wanderings and Scribblings; or Journal of a Journey South and West in May, June, and July, 1841," LOC.

45. Ibid.

46. African slaves, who seized the Spanish ship *Amistad* off the Cuban coast and sailed it to U.S. waters near Long Island. Former president John Quincy Adams successfully defended the mutinous slaves before the Supreme Court. Morrill encountered them as they briefly toured the Northeast, prior to sailing for Africa.

47. Morrill, "Wanderings."

48. Ibid.

49. Ibid.

50. Dr. Wilbur K. Jordan, "The Education of Justin Smith Morrill," Honors Day Address at University of Vermont, 1 May 1862, Vermont Historical Society.

51. Barbara York, "The Morrill Homestead," University of Vermont, 1983. The house became a National Historic Landmark in 1962 and is open for public tours.

52. York, "The Morrill Homestead"; interview with Gwenda Smith, Strafford historian and docent at the Morrill homestead, July 1995.

53. York, "The Morrill Homestead"; Harrison L. Flint, "Some Horticultural Activities of Justin Smith Morrill," *Arnoldia* 28 (7 June 1968): 41–52.

54. Plans at the Morrill home; interview with Gwenda Smith.

55. B. F. Tenney to Morrill, 3 October 1849; J. N. Morrill to Morrill, 22 August 1839; Morrill to Caira Langdon, n.d., Morrill Collection, Syracuse University.

56. Parker, *Morrill*, 51.

57. Ibid., 52–53; Ruth Swan to Mrs. Caleb Swan, 18 September 1849, Swan Collection, Massachusetts Historical Society; Morrill to Solomon Foot, 11 September 1854, LOC; A and H. S. Overholt to John Covode, 25 July 1862, Morrill Collection, Syracuse University.

58. Morrill to Dr. Caleb Swan, 31 January 1852, University of Vermont Library; Morrill to Henry Wardner, 20 August 1877, University of Vermont Library; Ruth Morrill to Dr. and Mrs. Swan, 14 March 1855; Ruth to Channing Morrill, 5 December 1864, Swan Collection, Massachusetts Historical Society.

59. Ruth to Dr. and Mrs. Swan, 14 March 1855, Swan Collection, Massachusetts Historical Society; Morrill to Ruth, 1 June 1856, LOC.

60. Morrill to Ruth, 1859–60s, LOC, for example.
61. None of the Morrill family papers mentions Ruth's epilepsy. Elderly Strafford residents, who can recall James and Louise and whose parents were Justin and Ruth's neighbors, do not recall ever hearing of Ruth's epilepsy.
62. Ruth to Dr. and Mrs. Swan, 14 March 1855, Swan Collection, Massachusetts Historical Society.
63. Barrett, "Early Life," 61–68, LOC.

2

MR. MORRILL GOES
TO WASHINGTON

Morrill transferred to the larger scene the experience and the motives of the
smaller one he had left, projecting into national affairs the habits and principles learned in the village. We shall probably understand him better . . .
if we think of him as applying to the great affairs of the nation the lessons
of his general store, his farm and his house.[1]

Biographer William Parker

Justin Morrill hardly had time to grieve for his losses. In 1854 the
country became embroiled, again, over slavery's extension into the
western territories. The Kansas-Nebraska Bill caused smoldering resent-
ments to flare up. Firebrands, on both sides, fanned the flames. This time
there would be no Henry Clay compromise to extinguish the fire.
Instead, zealots carried the Kansas spark to the halls of Congress. From
there it would soon spread across the entire country. The nation divided
north-south along sectional lines. The Whig Party divided with it and
succumbed to the change. From the Whig Party's ashes arose the
Republican Party uniting slavery's opponents from all factions. In
December 1855 Justin Morrill would join the battle line in Congress.
Although the fight against slavery occupied most of his time and energy
during his first term, he also led the battle against polygamy, the other
"twin pillar of barbarism."

In 1854 Andrew Tracy, representative from Vermont's Second
Congressional District, unexpectedly announced he would not seek a
second term. Surprised party leaders offered the nomination and their

support to Justin Morrill, although he had never held elected office beyond justice of the peace. Since the district voted Whig by a substantial margin, the party's nomination usually assured election. While contemplating his response, he surveyed friends who confirmed widespread support for his candidacy. Although he believed no one else "stood head and shoulders above all others," he still hesitated. Political office did not appeal to him, he said, and the blow to his pride a loss would cause made him reluctant. Reassurance from friends that he would easily be elected persuaded Morrill to run. The Whig Convention, meeting at White River on 27 July 1854, nominated Justin Morrill as its candidate for United States representative from Vermont's Second District.[2]

Although Morrill had never held important public office, he was no political novice. He had spent over 20 years studying and discussing issues with his father, Judge Harris, and his fellow townsmen at the general store. He had also been active in Whig party politics. In 1844, as chair of the Orange County Whig Committee, he engaged in brisk correspondence with the county Democratic chair J. W. D. Parker on topics for a "discussion of issues." After Parker disagreed with Morrill's choices, Morrill replied that political discussion without including those selected subjects would be like a "performance of the '*Tragedy of Hamlet*'—with the part of Hamlet omitted."[3] Apparently there was no performance with or without Hamlet as Morrill wrote Parker a few months later chiding him for backing out of the discussion again.[4]

By 1848 Morrill, a member of the state Whig Committee, had already developed a close relationship with the press, another lesson that would serve him well throughout his own political career. A political ally, Thomas Hale, editor of the Windsor *Journal*, asked Morrill's advice on responding to a Democrat who wanted to place an ad offering himself as a congressional candidate. Morrill suggested placing the ad with a disclaimer reading in part: "*[G]o ahead, Captain Partridge! you many drum on our end of the log, if you pay us pretty well in the 'hard,' and play on to them unappreciating doughfaced, grandam, locofoco friends of yours a little harder.*" He also promised to send Hale an article for his paper, if the state committee duties allowed the time.[5]

Justin Morrill was well-known in Whig circles by 1848. He corresponded with local Whig leaders throughout the state, advising them on the status of Orange County and the surrounding area's political leanings and soliciting the same information from them. He recalled later, "I was always ready to make a speech or write a political platform resolution, and after a time they began to expect them from me."[6] Morrill and Senator Solomon Foot frequently exchanged letters and developed a strong friendship. A letter from Vermont's other Senator William Upham asking Morrill to help thwart an opponent's attempt to block the senator's reelection shows Morrill's influence in state politics.[7]

Politics occupied much of Morrill's time in the late 1840s and early 1850s. Although he attended state and local political meetings, he refused all nominations to office. Meanwhile, he educated himself on the issues, later stating, "I realized that public question must have a little more serious study. I had always had in my library all I could afford, but now political economy had some attention besides other literature."[8] Any subject, personal or public, that caught his interest prompted him to read until he had mastered it. Morrill would continue to study economic questions after his election until he eventually became the acknowledged Congressional expert on tariffs.

By 1850 he had defined himself politically as a Webster Whig and a Free-Soil Whig. But, already, he favored compromise and reason over division and confrontation. Throughout his political career, he built friendships and sought common ground. In 1852 E. P. Walton, editor of the *Montpelier Watchman*, promised to support Morrill for lieutenant governor. Later in the year, Vermont Whigs selected Morrill as a delegate to the national convention in Baltimore that nominated Winfield Scott for president.[9]

Scott and the Whigs faced a nearly impossible challenge in 1852. Four years earlier, following a brief war, the vanquished Mexican government had ceded more than 500 thousand square miles of territory, including California, Nevada, Utah, and parts of Arizona and New Mexico, to United States. The acquisition reignited the always smoldering controversy over slavery in the territories. Previously, the Northwest Ordinance of 1787 had banned slavery from the Northwest Territory, but that was before cotton production had become a cornerstone of the southern economy. The Louisiana Purchase raised the question again. Henry Clay's Missouri Compromise of 1820 settled the immediate controversy by admitting Missouri as a slave state, Maine as a free state, and establishing 36 degrees 30 minutes as the dividing line between potentially slave and free territories in the Louisiana Purchase. Although the agreement completely satisfy neither North nor South, both sides accepted it.

By 1848 both South and North had become more rigid in their positions on slavery. In the South slavery was firmly intrenched. The Industrial

Revolution in England made the large scale production of cotton cloth feasible. The South was the primary cotton supplier for English mills and slaves were the labor force to produce the cotton. In the North, meanwhile, the anti-slavery sentiment had grown stronger. The abolitionists' movement, although never large, received more press coverage than their numbers would indicate. Abolitionists attacked slavery, not so much on legal grounds, but on emotional and moral ones. William Lloyd Garrison's *Liberator* and other newspapers condemned slavery as sinful, depicted slave owners as depraved, and portrayed them as representative of southern values. The South defended slavery as a positive good and accused northerners of inciting slave insurrection in the South.

The Missouri Compromise had created a shaky peace, at best, but one that both sides continued to respect. The peace also depended upon equilibrium in Congress. The North with its population advantage controlled the House of Representatives. The Senate was more balanced and southerners held enough key positions to thwart any attack on their "sacred rights."

The controversy over the Mexican War began before the war did. Northern Whigs condemned Democratic President James K. Polk for provoking a war, calling it a proslavery conspiracy to gain more territory. In 1846 Whigs gained control of Congress and passed a resolution declaring that President Polk had "unconstitutionally and unnecessarily" begun the war. Also in 1846, David Wilmot, a Pennsylvania Democratic congressman, proposed to ban slavery in any territory acquired from Mexico. The House passed the Wilmot Proviso, but the Senate killed it. Nevertheless, the South perceived the Proviso as a direct attack on its institutions and its rights.

The question of slavery's status in any new territory was definitely *not* resolved when President Polk endorsed the Treaty of Guadalupe Hidalgo, on 2 February 1848, ending the Mexican War. The United States promised to pay Mexico $15 million and assumed U.S. citizens' claims against that government for another $3.2 million. In return, Mexico ceded more than one-third of its territory, over one-half million square miles, to the United States. The southern-dominated Senate quickly approved the treaty.

Congress faced four alternatives for dealing with slavery in the newly acquired territory. Abolitionists, free-soilers, and most northern Whigs supported Wilmot's proposal to ban slavery in the new territory. John Calhoun and the southerners demanded their right to take their "property" (read slaves) into the new lands. Some people from both parties and both sections, including Secretary of State James Buchanan, recommended extending the Missouri Compromise line to the Pacific Ocean. The last group, headed by Democratic Presidential Nominee Lewis Cass, wanted the people in the territories or new states to decide for themselves ("popular sovereignty").

John Marshall's discovery of gold in California in January 1848 forced Congress to address immediately slavery's status in the Mexican Cession. More than 80 thousand immigrants flocked to California in 1849 alone. President Zachary Taylor advised Californians to apply for immediate statehood, bypassing the territorial stage and the controversy that went with it. When Congress convened in December 1849, the president urged California and New Mexico's admission as free states. If Congress followed the president's advice, the two new states would give free states a seventeen to fifteen advantage and the ability to control both houses of Congress. Southerners might allow California's admission, but only in exchange for a guarantee that slavery's future would be secure. But northern voters would have quickly replaced any congressman who offered such a guarantee. The two sides were at an impasse, with California's status in limbo, for eight months. Northerners, of both parties, were adamant that slavery would not extend into the new territory. Southerners threatened to secede if their perceived Constitutional property rights were not enforced.

In January 1850, after securing Daniel Webster's promise of support, Senator Henry Clay introduced eight resolutions designed to resolved the contentions that threatened the country. First, California would come into the Union as a free state. The rest of the Mexican Cession would have territorial governments, "without the adoption of any restriction or condition on the subject of slavery." The territorial legislatures would decide upon slavery's status in their territories. The next resolution fixed Texas' western boundary at about its present limits, gave a disputed area to New Mexico, and assumed responsibility for Texas' public debt. Then, Clay proposed the end of slave trade in the District of Columbia, but the continuation of slavery there. Another resolution would ban Congress from interfering with interstate slave trade. Clay last suggested a new Fugitive Slave Law that would allow slave owners to retrieve runaway slaves from the free states.[10]

The Congressional debate on Clay's resolutions involved the Senate's greatest orators and took more than eight months. Henry Clay offered the resolutions as a means of avoiding disunion and war. John Calhoun,

23

so sick that he had Senator James Mason read his speech, warned that equilibrium was essential to the continued union of North and South. He urged Congress to maintain that balance. Daniel Webster argued that environment would exclude slavery from the new territory and he "would not take pains to reaffirm an ordinance of nature nor to re-enact the will of God." Webster would not support a Wilmot Proviso, since it would serve no other purpose than to antagonize the South. William Seward called the resolutions "radically wrong and essentially vicious," and affirmed there was a "higher law than the Constitution." After six months of debate, during which both Senator Calhoun and President Taylor died, the Senate defeated Clay's resolutions.[11]

At this point, Senator Stephen Douglas stepped forward and took up the battle. Meanwhile, Millard Fillmore, who replaced Taylor as president, threw his support behind the resolutions. Whereas Clay bound his resolutions into an "Omnibus Bill," Douglas would offer separate bills. He pushed through a bill delineating Texas' western border, then another admitting California into the Union and establishing a territorial government in New Mexico. He also ushered through a new Fugitive Slave Law. Another measure allowed slavery to continue in the District of Columbia, but banned the slave trade there. Thus, by depending on ever-shifting coalitions, Douglas accomplished what Clay could not. President Fillmore quickly signed the bills into law. The total package became known as the Compromise of 1850 and it resolved the immediate sectional differences.[12]

One surprising result of the battle for the Compromise was the death of the Whig Party. During the battle to enact Clay's resolutions, the Whigs divided along sectional lines into pro-compromise (southern) and anti-compromise (northern) factions. Northern Whigs felt betrayed, especially over the more stringent Fugitive Slave Law. The Whig Party no longer spoke with one voice. So the party had little chance of success in the 1852 presidential election.

Morrill must have realized this at the nominating 1852 convention in Baltimore. While there Morrill's political idol Secretary of State Daniel Webster, who coveted the nomination for president, invited the young delegate for dinner. The food and wine were excellent. But, for Morrill, "the greatest treat was to hear Webster talk at his own table unreservedly." Webster's graceful movements and extensive knowledge impressed the younger man. Although the convention nominated Winfield Scott, Morrill continued to admire Webster even after he had become a senator himself.[13]

After returning home, Morrill worked diligently, but in vain, to elect Scott president. Even though Vermont voted for Scott, only three other states supported him. Franklin Pierce, the Democratic candidate, won in a landslide. Although not immediately apparent, the loss finished the Whigs as a national party. They would never compete in another presidential election.

After the Whig defeat in 1852, Morrill knew the party needed rejuvenating. Working quietly, he traveled around the state helping motivate and organize "something younger than the Fogies." In an 1853 letter to Judge Harris, Morrill cautioned his old friend not to be too optimistic about the party's chances. Although "we have roused the rascals to desperation and they bleed the promised officeholders sharply—so that it is asking possibly more than we can do to carry the thing clean."[14] Morrill's political stature had grown so much by 1853 that Walton considered him a possible candidate for the U.S. Senate in 1854. Morrill quickly asserted that he was not a candidate, and "[t]herein I hold myself lucky, as I shall not tax the mind of my friends to *blow me up*, nor the gas of my enemies to do that same in a less gracious manner."[15] Morrill would not try for the Senate, but circumstances moved him toward the House of Representatives.

So when the White River Whig Convention nominated Justin Morrill in 1854, it did not nominate a political novice. Expressing his views on the important issues of the day, candidate Morrill opposed admitting additional slave states into the Union or allowing slavery to spread into the territories. He supported changing the Fugitive Slave Law to ensure a jury trial and the right of *habeas corpus* for accused runaway slaves. He, also, suggested substituting money for the Navy's liquor rations and prohibiting "groggeries" near the Capitol in Washington.[16] The Montpelier *Watchman* considered him well-fitted for public service as a good speaker, a "liberal, honorable, and modest" politician, a gentleman, and "one of the cleverest fellows in the world." [17]

Despite his friends' assurances, Justin Morrill's election was not a certainty. Zealous free-soilers, unconvinced by his statement against the spread of slavery, bolted the convention and selected O. L. Shafter as their candidate. The Democrats nominated J. W. D. Parker. Doctor Powers, who was the force behind Maine's law prohibiting the sale of alcohol, backed Shafter. Rumors calling Morrill a "rum-seller" and a heavy drinker gained enough credence that he felt the need to reassure Senator Foot the charges were not true. Morrill believed Powers cost him

200–300 votes. Since there was not a designated election day for the entire district, votes trickled in. With the votes in four towns still to be counted, Morrill led. But he was certain those towns would go Democratic by sufficient margin to prevent his receiving a clear majority. When all votes were in, however, Parker had 5,848, Shafter 2,473, and Morrill 8,380. Justin Morrill was elected representative by 59 votes. This was his first of many election victories and the last for the Whig Party in Vermont.[18]

Although Judge Harris lived to see his protege elected to Congress in September 1854, he died before Morrill took office in December 1855. Harris' death deprived Congressman Morrill of his mentor's sage advice, but the skills and lessons Harris had taught served Morrill well in Congress. Joining Morrill in the Thirty-fourth Congress were several other first-time members, including two who would become Morrill's close associates and friends, Ohio's John Sherman and Indiana's Schuyler Colfax.

The new Congress promised to be a lively one, dominated by slavery's status in Kansas Territory. The previous Congress had again brought the slavery issue to the forefront. Democratic Senator Stephen Douglas had presented a bill to organize the Nebraska Territory into two potential states and allow the new states' citizens to choose or deny slavery, through "popular sovereignty." To gain the southern support needed to pass the measure, Douglas added a statement nullifying the Missouri Compromise of 1820. He argued the Compromise of 1850, which allowed New Mexico and Utah Territories to decide slavery for themselves, had already voided the earlier agreement. Whigs and northern Democrats who had supported the 1850 Compromise felt betrayed. But Douglas steered the Kansas-Nebraska bill through Congress and President Franklin Pierce signed it into law.

During the almost fourteen months between Morrill's election and his first session of Congress, northern Whigs, Free-Soilers, northern Democrats and other anti-slavery factions united into the Republican Party. The new party was born as a "free soil" reaction to the Kansas-Nebraska Act and the repeal of the Missouri Compromise. Morrill's ability to seek common ground undoubtedly helped ease the Republican Party's birth in Vermont. He and the state's other Whigs seemed to transition into the new party without rift or schism. The Thirty-fourth Congress, which opened on 3 December 1855, included 108 anti-Nebraska or Republican members (dedicated to preventing the spread of slavery into the territories), 83 Democrats (most of whom were pro-slavery southerners), and 43 American Party or "Know-Nothings" (on both sides of the slavery issue). Historian Allan Nevins described Washington in December 1855 as "a boiling caldron of party antagonisms," where members of Congress gathered in "sectional" boardinghouses and spoke "lurid words" for the extremists of both sides.[19]

Morrill opted for one of the "sectional" boardinghouses. He later recalled, "Party feeling on the slavery question was intense and was a wall of separation which kept asunder not only political parties at Washington but divided society."[20] Ruth, still grieving over young Justin's death, spent the winter at her father's home in Easton, Massachusetts.[21] Senator Foot suggested that Morrill joined him and other New Englanders at Mrs. Curtis' boardinghouse, where a comfortable room and a "fair table" cost twelve to sixteen dollars a week, depending upon the size of the room. Senator Foot stressed that Morrill must be there for the opening of the session because every vote would count.[22]

The Thirty-fourth Congress' opening session proved Foot correct. Electing a speaker of the House created an immediate stalemate. Instead of seeking a compromise candidate, each side chose someone unacceptable to the other. The Democrats, claiming to be "conservative in their principles, policy and men," selected William A. Richardson of Illinois, who had steered the hated Kansas-Nebraska Act through the House. While the Republicans, whom Morrill described as "almost hopelessly divided as to men and measures," backed Nathaniel P. Banks of Massachusetts, an ex-Democrat who became a Republican in protest of the Kansas-Nebraska Act. The Know-Nothings, whose primary agenda was anti-Catholic and anti-immigrant, settled on Henry M. Fuller. Neither side was willing to ease its position. By the sixty-eighth ballot, on Christmas Eve, Banks had 101 votes, Richardson 72, and Fuller 31. Eleven votes went to other candidates. No one had the necessary majority.[23]

Morrill followed the party leadership and consistently voted for Banks. Although acknowledging that he felt "green" because he lacked legislative experience, he was grateful several others were as green and "rather bigger fools" then he. Morrill believed the new Republican members "largely compensated by fresh enthusiasm and persistent determination." His constituents supported this persistence. One voter admonished him to "[s]tick to Banks at all events, even if you vote for him as many months as you have already voted days. Better let Congress live and die unorganized than to be organized by the choice of a

Nebraska man. . . . The question may as well be decided now as at any future time whether there is a North or not."[24]

And persist they did. The fruitless balloting continued. Republicans attempted to keep the House in session until they elected their man. Morrill described a session that began at noon and continued until after six the next morning. He had voted with the other Republicans against adjournment. In a letter to Ruth, he wrote, "Mr. Cullen of Delaware, Mr. Bowie of Maryland and Campbell of Kentucky have been very drunk and others a little drunk. We have kept good-natured, silly and noisy." The good-naturedness turned hostile, however, when a "little scene" occurred that led to "very disgraceful confusion."[25]

Since the House could conduct no business until it elected a speaker, members found a new way to insult each other. Each day when the clerk called the roll, members would "make a personal explanation," which became an attack on the opposition candidate. Morrill recounted, "Whenever the candidate was gored so as to rise and explain, his tormentors seemed to enjoy it hugely."[26] Eventually, members decided the candidates should answer a series of questions to show their suitability for speaker. Each side used this opportunity to further degrade the opposition. The questions generally focused on slavery, the equality of the races, or the future status of slavery in the country. South Carolina's Preston Brooks reflected the depth of southern feelings: "We are standing upon slave territory, surrounded by slave States, and pride, honor, patriotism all command us, if a battle is to be fought, to fight it out here upon this floor."[27]

Finally, after two months and more than one hundred ballots, both sides relented and agreed to elect the speaker by plurality instead of a majority of votes. Thus, on 2 February, on the 133d ballot, Banks received 103 votes to 100 votes for William Aiken of South Carolina, who had replaced Richardson. All Banks' votes were from free-states and all votes for Aiken, except one, came from slave-states. Aiken attempted to soothe embittered feelings by claiming the privilege of escorting Banks to the speaker's chair.[28] Describing the victory to Ruth, Morrill wrote:

Tell your father we didn't "flunk out" as he predicted we should. Nevertheless it has been achieved only by the most arduous effort you can conceive. We had to meet able, adroit, bold, cunning, and reckless forces. They fought us at every step, and even after Banks was elected continued

28

the fight, a portion of them, for two hours like graceless, bully black-guards.[29]

Morrill later described this battle for House speaker as "the first gust, the large pelting drops, that preceded the storm of 1861."[30]

There was little chance that embittered feelings would stay soothed for long. With a speaker finally elected, Congress next had to confront conflicting petitions for Kansas statehood. Both North and South viewed Kansas as critical to the battle over slavery. Northerners would fight to keep slavery from spreading into the territories. Southerners would fight to exercise their property rights in the national domain. Describing the atmosphere, Nevins wrote, "Dark stormclouds hung over" the entire country, "and livid lightning shook a portentous finger across the recently smiling landscape."[31]

Both sides had sought an advantage in Kansas even before the Kansas-Nebraska bill became law. Eli Thayer incorporated the Massachusetts Emigrant Aid Society to encourage and help free-soil settlers move to Kansas. Although the Emigrant Aid Society only helped resettle 1,240 people, the movement outraged southerners. Southerners countered with Blue Lodges, Social Bands, and Sons of the South, groups sworn to uphold their "property" rights. Slave-holding Missourians had a special interest in the territory: the Missouri counties with the most slaves were those along the Kansas border. Hundreds of Missourians slipped across the border and laid claim to the land, even before it became legally available.[32]

In autumn 1854, Kansas voters tested "popular sovereignty." Although Territorial Governor Andrew H. Reeder estimated fifteen hundred to two thousand eligible voters in the territory, 2,871 people voted in the election. One person claimed that seventeen hundred Missourians crossed the border and voted illegally. The elected legislature was overwhelmingly pro-slavery. This body met at Lecompton and drew up a state constitution embracing slavery and refused Kansans the right to accept or reject the document. Outraged free-soilers reacted by forming their own antislavery government in Topeka with a proposed constitution that condemned slavery. Both sides petitioned Congress for statehood under their respective constitutions. President Pierce and later President James Buchanan favored the Lecompton constitution and encouraged Congress to accept it. The Republican Party was born to oppose slavery in Kansas.[33]

Describing the situation, Morrill later said, "For sixty years the slave-holders had regarded the exaggeration of State rights as the summit of statesmanship and the all-sufficient shield of slavery." Southerners defied "the rapidly accumulating and crushing opinion of the civilized world" and placed slavery under the "ark of safety of states' rights." Because cotton production exhausted the soil, slavery depended upon new territory to survive. Therefore:

> when the enlightened conscience of the North would no longer prostitute the power of the National Government to the extension of slavery . . . then the South determined to wreck the fairest fabric of human government the world has yet known and to trust to the anarchy for the preservation of their domination over the African race.[34]

This was the predicament Justin Morrill and his colleagues confronted after their own bitter struggle in electing the speaker of the House.

Kansan William Hutchinson, who expected to become senator under the extralegal Topeka constitution, sought Morrill's support. Hutchinson asked for materials to argue his case to the voters and help in securing Kansas' statehood as a free state. He indicated that Vermont and Orange County were well-represented in the territory.[35] Another letter from Randolph, Vermont, also suggested that several local residents had moved to Kansas. Trying to encourage even more Vermonters to go, Morrill apparently suggested that Governor Erastus Fairbanks give free train tickets to free-soil settlers who would move. But the governor considered the idea impractical.[36]

Vermont's citizens left little doubt about their position. Many wrote Morrill, even before he took his seat, expressing their outrage. They would fight, if necessary, to keep slavery from spreading. Vermonters strongly urged Morrill to unite with other antislavery men and oppose slavery's expansion. Samuel Whitcomb, a constituent, told Morrill if northern representatives held firm and 80–90 pro-slavery members walked out, "Let them *go* and *good* riddance it will be. We shall never see a *better time* for testing the strength of our government." John Kimball of Putney probably spoke for many of his neighbors when he wrote, "Freedom and Union must stand together or fall together—the Union is good for nothing without Freedom, nor Freedom without the Union."[37]

Neither Vermonters, Kansans, nor members of Congress sought common-ground. Bloodshed by both sides, including John Brown's massacre of five pro-slavery settlers at Pottawatomie and the slavery sympathizers raid on "free-soil" Lawrence, spilled over into Congress. On May 19 Massachusetts Senator Charles Sumner unleashed a diatribe entitled "The Crime Against Kansas" on the floor of the Senate. His vitriolic remarks on the South and slavery inflamed even some passive members of Congress. Three days later South Carolina's Congressman Preston Brooks fulfilled his promise to carry his fight to the floors of Congress. While Sumner was sitting at his Senate desk, Brooks approached and caned Sumner into unconsciousness. Southerners cheered and northerners were appalled. Members carried weapons into Congressional chambers. Morrell later recalled, "One day I heard Mr. Spinner . . . offer to make a wager that there were not less than three hundred loaded pistols in the hall and galleries of the House." Morrill described the atmosphere as intense and told his wife he expected "scenes of great turbulence." "No one from the North will bate his breath for fear of bullies, however, and blow for blow in all cases will be given." But he asked Ruth not to worry, "I shan't run, arm, nor kill anybody, and I don't intend to be whipt or shot."[38]

While awaiting the decision on whether the House would expel Brooks,[39] Justin Morrill made his first congressional speech on 28 June 1856. Although he had studied the great orators, including his hero Webster, Morrill was not a great speaker himself. Biographer Parker noted, "he lacked the voice, the action, the power of utterance, and the love of forensic combat to make him an ideal speaker."[40] But, his speeches, which he read, were carefully written and his arguments well supported. Like Webster, he considered the Union sacred, but he was no fire-breathing abolitionist. Entitled "Admission of Kansas as a Free State into the Union," the speech began with conciliatory words as Morrill did not wish to "plant a thorn in the side" of the southern states. He affirmed the glory of Virginia, Kentucky, New England, and the "western empire" as American glory. While both North and South had earned praise, both also deserved admonishment over slavery's introduction and spread in the United States. Southerners owned and kept slaves, but northerners had brought them from Africa and had bought and sold them. Still, "from the clearest light we have from above, from history, from experience, from the combined testimony of good men of all ages, slavery is wrong." While he did not propose interfering with the consciences or rights of other men, he would oppose slavery's extension.[41]

He then presented his arguments for the admission of Kansas as a free state. The first question he considered was "Would the state have a republican form of government?" Since the Topeka convention used the U.S. Constitution as its model, Morrill doubted that anyone would fault this constitution for lacking "*anything* of republicanism." Next, he addressed the qualities of Kansans themselves. Did they have sufficient numbers and intelligence to form a state and be good citizens? By comparing Connecticut and New York, Morrill showed that small states could govern just as effectively as large ones. Seven states had been admitted with fewer people than Kansas had at that time. So, he stressed, the territory had enough people and no one questioned their intelligence. He had little doubt that, if admitted to the Union under the Topeka constitution, Kansans "would sustain their position with safety and honor to themselves and us."[42]

Opponents, seeking to delay action on the Topeka constitution, had attacked the veracity of newspapers reporting extensive voter fraud in the general election and widespread support among Kansans for the free-soil constitution. Morrill, who depended on newspaper backing at home, defended the press against charges of inaccurate reporting. He claimed, "There is no class of men whose prosperity so greatly depends upon their being scrupulously accurate in their general statements of facts and occurrences as the makers of newspapers, and none more truthful and reliable."[43] This was an obvious overstatement, especially in 1856 when newspapers were notoriously partisan. Historian David Potter said "Bleeding Kansas" was the antislavery press' "supreme achievement." "Here they attained some of their most striking effects; here, also, they practiced some of their most palpable and most successful distortions of the evidence."[44] Besides the newspaper accounts, Morrill continued, official information confirmed the voter fraud.

In comparison, according to him, the pro-slavery Lecompton constitution, written by fraudulently elected legislators, was "an open and palpable violation of the Constitution." Calling the entire document "unworthy of an American origin," Morrill specifically condemned provisions that made sworn support for the Fugitive Slave Law a prerequisite for voting, authorized imprisonment for antislavery speeches or written articles, and forbade a person opposed to slavery from serving on juries. Such laws, he asserted, would make the "blood of a rebel glow in [the] veins" of any House member, North or South.[45]

Trying to keep his argument political instead of sectional, Morrill blamed Franklin Pierce's Democratic administration for the troubles in Kansas. The administration's policies, including its defense of slavery, alienated other nations and provoked "hatred and incurable irritation abroad, without securing love or respect at home." If the United States had to defend itself from some foreign enemy, Morrill believed only Russia, "the conqueror of Hungary," would be our "cordial friend." He concluded his attack on the Democrats and closed in a more conciliatory tone, appealing to House members' sense of nationalism: "If we cannot add a cubit to our own stature, we can raise and elevate that of the nation by an act at once just and generous, and which promises harmony and repose to the country."[46]

Although Morrill delivered the speech late in the afternoon, when members were eager to vote on Kansas statehood, he was pleased with the result. He told Ruth portions of the speech "kept the House in good humor" and his friends in Congress were "entirely satisfied" with his "maiden effort."[47] His speech reflected both his and his constituents' views and those of most Republicans. The full House did approve statehood under the Topeka constitution on 3 July, but the bill died in the Senate. Kansas continued to dominate proceedings until 1858 when Indiana Senator William H. English proposed a compromise. Kansans would vote on the entire Lecompton constitution. If they accepted it, the territory would immediately become a state, get the standard 3,988,868-acre land grant, plus a 5 percent bonus from an upcoming sale of 2,000,000 acres. If voters rejected the document, statehood would wait until the population reached that of a congressional district, probably about two more years. Voters rejected the Lecompton constitution 11,812 to 1,926. The vote delayed Kansas statehood until 29 January 1861, when she became the nation's thirty-fourth state.

While the struggle in Kansas still raged, another event made the situation even more volatile. On 6 March 1857, the Supreme Court ruled on the Dred Scott case. Scott, a slave, had sued for his freedom on the grounds that his owner had taken him into territories and states that prohibited slavery. The Supreme Court, dominated by southern members, ruled that Scott could not sue his owner, because a slave was not, nor could ever be, a citizen of the United States. The Court further stated that it was unconstitutional for Congress to exclude slavery from the territories. Northerners reacted to the decision with disbelief and then outrage. They believed the Supreme Court had conspired with incoming President James Buchanan and southern slave owners to spread slavery into areas where it was previously prohibit. To counter the Court's decision, Republican leaders declared the statements concerning slavery in the territories as *obiter dictum*, or an opinion given on a subject not before the Court and therefore without the force of law. This allowed opponents to ignore the ruling without feeling they were breaking the law.[48]

Meanwhile, Morrill introduced his first legislation. The measure had nothing to do with Kansas, slavery, tariffs, or land-grant colleges. Instead he proposed that the federal government suppress polygamy among the Latter-Day Saints, or Mormons, in Utah Territory. In June 1856 he reported his bill from the Committee on Territories, on which he served, to the entire House. His supporting argument focused on Congress' power to make laws governing the territories. Since polygamy was a moral outrage, Congress could ban the practice without violating the freedom of religion clause of the Constitution. "There is no purpose to interfere with the rights of freedom of religion, nor to intermeddle with the rights of conscience, but the sole design is to punish gross offenses whether in secular or ecclesiastical garb; to prevent practices which outrage the moral sense of the civilized world."[49] At the time, however, there was little public interest in polygamy, Utah Territory, or the Mormons. So the House referred the bill to the Committee of the Whole where it died.[50]

The following January, during the House debate on appropriations for Utah, Morrill asked President James Buchanan to submit to Congress records concerning events in Utah. But the president did not respond. On 23 February 1957, as the House neared the conclusion of discussions on Utah appropriations, Morrill spoke again of the misconduct and atrocities in the territory. This time he focused on Territorial Governor and Mormon leader Brigham Young and his followers' disregard and defiance of federal laws. Morrill referred to an 1851 report by "Chief Justice Branderberry, Associate Justice Brocchus, and Secretary Harris," federal officials appointed to the territory. The officials reported the Mormon church had usurped federal authority and controlled territorial legislative and judicial functions. The report claimed, "The Mormons are quite as hostile to the republican form of government as they are to the usual forms of Christianity," and only a "military force" could remove Young as territorial governor. Although Morrill acknowledged these charges once had been considered "too extravagant for belief," subsequent information from official correspondence and non-Mormons, or "Gentiles," who had visited Utah, substantiated the report.[51]

He then cited instances where utterances by Young and specific territorial laws defied federal authority and directives. Morrill had taken time to study Salt Lake City newspapers and Utah's territorial laws for examples. He said a former Army officer told him Brigham Young asserted that "God Almighty made him Governor; that the [federal] commission doesn't do it." Reportedly, Young had also said, "I shall act as Governor until God Almighty says to me, Brigham, you needn't be Governor any longer." Morrill then quoted one of Young's sermons, reprinted in the *Deseret News*, "I say, as the Lord lives, we are bound to become a sovereign state in the Union, or an independent nation by ourselves, and let them drive us from this place if they can; they cannot do it."[52]

Territorial laws, according to Morrill, proved that Young intended to consolidate powers reserved for the federal government into his own hands. He had formed a battalion of "life guards," which aspired to a "Napoleonic model" and "subject, at all times, to the call of the Governor and Lieutenant General." The governor also controlled the manufacture of all "ardent spirits." One law specifically empowered Brigham Young "to establish, regulate, and control ferries and bridges on Weber and Bear rivers." Another forbade residents from paying attorneys. Others gave the governor right to dispose of property, timber, and water, all rights specifically reserved for Congress. Morrill also accused the Mormons of African and Indian slavery.[53]

Finally, after devoting three-quarters of his speech to the Mormons' defiance of federal laws, Morrill reached the heart of his argument: polygamy, "a Mohammedan barbarism revolting to the civilized world." According to him, the Mormons practiced polygamy "in its most disgusting form, including in its slimy folds sisters, mothers, and daughters; and in order that no element of cruelty and loathsomeness may be wanting, it includes facility of divorce." He believed the practice degraded women to the level of animals. Citing a passage from *The Book of Mormon* (a copy of which is still in his personal library) limiting a man to one wife and no "concubines," Morrill asserted the Saints had later adopt polygamy to satisfy the "appetites of the lusty Joseph Smith, Jr., and his followers." Polygamy, according to Morrill, had no more protection under the Constitution's freedom of religion clause than cannibalism or infanticide.[54]

He concluded that he hoped Utah's residents would correct these transgressions and affronts to the Constitution. If they did not, he encouraged Congress to act by repealing offensive laws and even reducing the size of Utah Territory. Congress might then divide the remainder among other territories or abandon the residents to "fight out their own independence and salvation."[55]

Because of the timing and Morrill's inexperience, the speech had little effect. By delivering the speech during deliberation on Utah's appropriations, he hoped to persuade the House to withhold funds until the territorial government complied with all federal laws. That motion failed, as did another to halt pay and mileage allowance for the territorial legislature.[56]

Although his speech had little impact in the House, his constituents liked it. One Vermonter thanked him for bringing the Utah atrocities to light. Another voter compared polygamy to slavery and added "before Heaven they are, both, as bad as evil can make them." Yet another constituent considered Young guilty of "treason and high crimes of misdemeanor against the morals, against society and against the Gov[ernment]."[57]

Later in 1857, as the public became more aware of events and practices in Utah, pressure forced President Buchanan to appoint three new federal judges, a marshal, a territorial secretary, a new superintendent of Indian affairs, and a new territorial governor to replace Young, whose term had expired. The president also dispatched 2,500 troops to ensure the new officials' safety and enforce their authority. The Mormons amassed about 2,000 territorial militiamen to repel the invading army. The federal troops settled into winter camp before reaching Utah. Meanwhile, at Mountain Meadows, Mormon zealots and their Indian allies slaughtered 120 immigrants, including women and children, passing through Utah on their way to California. Twenty years later John D. Lee, who led and planned the murders and the only person convicted of the crime, was executed in Mountain Meadows. After the Mountain Meadows Massacre, Brigham Young decided further resistance was futile and mediated a settlement of hostilities. In 1858 Albert Cumming became Utah's territorial governor, but Brigham Young still held the real authority.[58]

Although the federal government had asserted nominal control of Utah Territory, Justin Morrill continued his moral crusade against polygamy there. On 15 February 1860, he introduced another bill to prohibit polygamy and annul several Utah territorial laws. *The Great Salt Lake City Mountaineer* questioned Morrill's avowed friendship for Utah and predicted the passage of his bill would put the entire territory "to fire and sword." The measure easily passed through the House by a vote of 149–60, but died in the Senate.[59]

Finally, in 1862, Morrill pushed his third anti-polygamy bill through Congress. President Abraham Lincoln signed the bill into law on 1 July

1862. But the law was meaningless without an army to enforce it and Lincoln would not divert soldiers from fighting rebels to Utah to battle Mormons. So even though illegal, polygamy continued among the Saints. In 1885 Amos Lawrence and Eli Thayer, powers behind the New England Emigrant Aid Company that helped enflame Kansas thirty years earlier, wrote Morrill offering to send "bona fide settlers" to Utah to "put down Mormonism forthwith." Morrill apparently did not rise to the challenge. The Church of the Latter-Day Saints did not relinquish the practice of polygamy until 1890. Utah became a state six years later on 4 January 1896.[60]

Morrill left no insightful letter explaining his passionate crusade against polygamy. Perhaps, he was simply responding to the desires of his constituents. Maybe he was motivated by his own sense of moral outrage. Most likely, this proud son of Vermont was determined to erase the perceived stain fellow Vermonters Brigham Young and Joseph Smith had placed on his state's reputation.

Although Morrill considered himself "green" when he entered Congress in December 1855, he worked hard and learned fast. He had little impact in his first term, but he had established himself and was poised to make a difference in his second. In September 1856, his constituents in Vermont's Second District expressed their approval of and faith in Morrill by an 8,000-vote margin for reelection. In his second term he would begin to find his niche as Congress' expert on tariffs.

Notes

1. Parker, *Morrill*, 83–84.
2. Morrill to William Upham, 3 July 1854, Morrill Collection, Vermont Historical Society; James Barrett "Justin Smith Morrill."
3. Morrill to J. W. D. Parker, 2 August 1844, LOC.
4. Morrill to Parker, 30 October 1844, LOC.
5. Morrill to Thomas Hale, 19 June 1848, LOC.
6. Parker, *Morrill*, 39.
7. William Upham to Morrill, 23 September 1848; Morrill to Portus Baxter, 8 June 1849; Morrill to Solomon Foot, 20 September 1850, LOC.
8. Parker, *Morrill*, 47–48.
9. Morrill to Ruth Morrill, 13 June 1852, cited in Parker, *Morrill*, 53; Morrill to Sen Solomon Foot, 25 July 1852, Morrill Collection, Vermont Historical Society.
10. David M. Potter, *The Impending Crisis, 1848–1861* (New York: Harper and Row, 1963), 90–120, has an excellent discussion on the 1850 Compromise.
11. Ibid.

12. Ibid.

13. Morrill to Ruth Morrill, 13 June 1852, cited in Parker, *Morrill,* 53; Morrill to Sen. Solomon Foot, 25 July 1852, Morrill Collection, Vermont Historical Society.

14. Morrill to Harris, 19 August 1853, LOC.

15. Morrill to Walton, 14 March 1853, LOC.

16. Morrill to S. Smith, 29 August 1854, printed in *The Vermonter,* January 1899, LOC.

17. Parker, *Morrill,* 59.

18. Morrill to Solomon Foot, 11 September 1854, Morrill Collection, Vermont Historical Society; Parker, *Morrill,* 60; P. T. Washburn to Morrill, 24 July 1854, LOC.

19. Allan Nevins, *Ordeal of the Union: A House Dividing, 1852–1857* (New York: Charles Scribner's Sons, 1947), 413.

20. Morrill, speech, "Some Recollections of Congress," delivered at Strafford, October 1875, LOC.

21. Morrill to Solomon Foot, 18 October 1855, LOC.

22. Solomon Foot to Morrill, quoted in Parker, *Morrill,* 62.

23. Nevins, *Ordeal of the Union,* 413–14; Morrill, speech, "Some Recollections of Congress."

24. Morrill, speech, "Some Recollections of Congress"; P. H. White to Morrill, 29 December 1855, LOC.

25. Morrill to Ruth Morrill, 10 January 1856, LOC.

26. Morrill, speech, "Some Recollections of Congress."

27. Ibid.

28. Nevins, *Ordeal of the Union,* 415–16; James M. McPherson, *The Battle Cry of Freedom* (New York: Oxford University Press, 1988), 144.

29. Morrill to Ruth Morrill, 3 February 1856, LOC.

30. Morrill, speech, "Some Recollections of Congress."

31. Nevins, *Ordeal of the Union,* 121.

32. McPherson, *Battle Cry of Freedom,* 145–46; Coy F. Cross II, *Go West, Young Man!* (Albuquerque: University of New Mexico Press, 1995), 80.

33. McPherson, *Battle Cry of Freedom,* 147–48; Cross, *Go West, Young Man!,* 85–90.

34. Parker, *Morrill,* 68.

35. William Hutchinson to Morrill, 29 December 1855, LOC.

36. J. K. Parish to Morrill, 6 February 1856; Governor Erastus Fairbanks to Morrill, 31 March 1856, LOC.

37. Samuel Whitcomb to Morrill, 22 November and 17 December 1855; A. Underwood to Morrill, 16 December 1855; Pliny H. White to Morrill, 29 December 1855; John Kimball to Morrill, 4 January 1856, LOC; Parker, *Morrill,* 63.

38. Morrill to Ruth Morrill, 22 May and 1 June 1856, LOC; Potter, *The Impending Crisis,* 209–11.

39. Congress fined Brooks $300, but allowed him to keep his seat. Morrill wrote Ruth, "They fined Brooks $300 for the assault on Sumner when if Sumner had beaten one of Brook's negroes as bad they would likely have fined him $1000 and imprisoned him to boot." Brooks then voluntarily resigned. His district, however, promptly reelected him and returned him to the House.

40. Parker, *Morrill,* 80.

41. Morrill, speech, "Admission of Kansas as a Free State into the Union," delivered in the House of Representatives, 28 June 1856, LOC.

42. Ibid.

43. Ibid.

44. Potter, *The Impending Crisis,* 218.

45. Morrill, speech, "Admission of Kansas."

46. Ibid.

47. Morrill to Ruth Morrill, 29 June 1856, LOC.

48. McPherson, *Battle Cry of Freedom,* 170–81.

49. Parker, *Morrill,* 83.

50. Randal Leigh Hoyer, "The Gentleman From Vermont: The Career of Justin S. Morrill in the United States House of Representatives" (Ph.D. diss., Michigan State University, 1974), 34–35.

51. Morrill, speech, "Utah Territory and its Laws—Polygamy and its License," delivered in the House of Representatives, 23 February 1857, LOC.

52. Ibid.

53. Ibid.

54. Ibid.

55. Ibid.

56. Hoyer, "Gentleman from Vermont," 40–41.

57. George F. Houghton to Morrill, 17 April 1857; C. Coolidge to Morrill, 27 April 1857; Thomas Kendrick to Morrill, 1 June 1857, LOC.

58. Kenneth M. Stampp, *America in 1857: A Nation on the Brink* (New York: Oxford University Press, 1990), 196–208.

59. Hoyer, "Gentleman from Vermont," 43–44; "Mr. Morrill on Polygamy, *Great Salt Lake City Mountaineer,* 31 March 1860, LOC.

60. Amos Lawrence to Morrill, 27 January 1885, LOC.

3

THE MORRILL TARIFF

The sole object of the tariff is to tax the produce of foreign industry with a view to promoting American industry.[1]

Henry Clay

During Morrill's second term in Congress the federal government confronted a problem unique to the nineteenth century: the Treasury had too much money. From the Republic's birth through the nineteenth century, tariffs and land sales were the federal government's primary source of income. The current tariff, enacted in 1846, charged 30 percent duty on most items. The country had prospered since 1846 and the federal revenue had exceeded expectations. To help eliminate the surplus in 1857, Congress proposed to expand the list of duty-free items and reduce the duty on most others. But Morrill objected. He and other protectionists, in the tradition of Henry Clay, believed the tariff should have another function besides financing the federal government: protecting America's fledgling industries from unfair foreign competition.[2]

On 6 February 1857, during the debate on a bill to solve the Treasury's excess money problem, Morrill spoke against the measure. He acknowledged the need to reduce the federal income. The American government should be based on "economy and republican simplicity." "The habit of reckless extravagance becomes as chronic with Governments as with individuals; and an excess of prosperity is an ordeal quite as severe for the one as the other. . . . An overflowing Treasury contains only one drop less of misery than an empty one."[3]

While supporting the bill in principle, Morrill objected to certain provisions. He criticized ad valorem duties based on an item's invoiced value. These, he believed, led to "systematic frauds" and provided the least protection when it was most needed, during times of low prices. Specific duties or fixed charges per unit, on the other hand, were "uniform and certain" for both revenue and protection.[4]

His chief concern, and that of his constituents, was the decrease in duties on wool and woolens. Originally, the bill allowed wool costing more that fifty cents or less than twenty cents a pound to be duty-free. This would provide cheap wool for blankets and fine wool for high priced fabrics. Medium wools, the grade most produced in the United States, would still pay a 30 percent duty. Concerned that unscrupulous shippers would tamper with their wool to make it fit into the duty-free category, Morrill suggested a 30 percent duty on wool "changed in its character for the purpose of evading duty." The bill's author, Lewis D. Campbell of Ohio, then proposed a 10 percent duty for raw wool and 30 percent for woolens. Morrill argued the duties should be the same, manufacturers needed protecting less than the growers.[5]

Morrill offered an amendment decreasing the maximum duty-free price for course wool from twenty cents to ten and excluding shoddy wool and pelts from duty-free status. The House adopted this amendment and he voted for the bill. The Senate, however, removed the clause concerning shoddy wool and pelts and raised the upper limit on course wool back to twenty cents per pound. A joint conference committee accepted the Senate version. When the House voted on the revised bill, Morrill voted against it. Despite his opposition the House approved the bill and it became law in March 1857.[6]

Protectionism did not begin with Justin Morrill. Indeed, protectionism's history preceded that of the Republic. But Henry Clay gave it credence and made it a national issue. Clay led the battle for the 1816 Tariff Act, the first bill that placed protection first and revenue second in importance. Protection reached its pre-Civil War zenith in 1828 in what opponents dubbed the "Tariff of Abominations." Protection continued as the tariff's primary role until 1846. In December 1845, Treasury Secretary Robert J. Walker, a free-trade advocate, presented a "revenue" tariff proposal to Congress that would reduce duties to "the lowest rate that would yield the largest amount of revenue." Although the 1846 Walker Tariff was moderately protective in its effect, contemporaries considered it the "nearest approach to free trade the United States had known since Jefferson's Presidency."[7]

Morrill accepted Henry Clay's philosophy on the protective tariff. At the 1843 District Whig Convention he served on the resolutions committee that condemned any treaty with England lowering tariff rates and recommended arrangements that would "provide a home supply and a home market."[8] In 1844 his Orange County Whig resolutions committee advocated higher tariffs to protect Vermont wool. Later as chair, Orange County Whig Committee, he challenged the Democratic Party chairman to debate the tariff issue.[9] Vermonters as owners of over one million sheep in 1850 had a personal interest in the subject. The sheep's owners and the manufacturers who converted the wool to woolens wanted their industry protected from cheap foreign competition. Morrill, representing both his own and his constituents' views, remained a steadfast proponent of protection throughout his political career. After a dozen years in Congress, he wrote, "The record will show that I never have touched the subject of wool in the Tariff where I did not give it greater protection than then existed."[10]

In 1883 when Harvard University students asked about his position of the tariff, he replied that a protective tariff was one of the "most potent means" of promoting "intellectual advancement of our people." It diversified employment and increased knowledge and wealth. Also, protection helped the country avoid trading handmade goods for machine-made ones. While admitting free-trade was a "captivating abstraction," he believed it had been a sorry failure in practice. He concluded that any country that did not rely on its own home manufacturers would become "an inferior servant of some other wiser and more prosperous people."[11]

Morrill's opposition to the 1857 Tariff Act, therefore, was in keeping with his values and his constituents' desires. Unfortunately, for the country, the economic boom that had induced Congress to pass the 1857 Tariff depended on exceptional conditions. California had fueled the nation's economy with $640 million in gold. In 1854, just when the gold output began to slow, the Crimean War, involving England, France and Russia, began. The war delivered a blow to Europe's industry and a boon to New England's. Also, the conflict prevented Russia from exporting wheat, which bolstered American wheat sales. American industry and railroad construction expanded beyond immediate demand. Speculation ran rampant. Between 1843 and 1857 banknote circulation increased from $58 million to $214 million and private indebtedness grew from

$254 million to $684 million. Foreign commercial indebtedness reached $394 million in 1857. Economic historian Edward Stanwood summed up conditions: "While the country was thus buying abroad much more than it paid for, it was overinvesting at home."[12]

By 1857 the California gold supply had dropped sharply. The European war was over, manufacturing had resumed, and the demand for American products decreased. Russia again competed with American farmers in the world wheat market. Railroad stock, which had become overinflated by construction dollars, began to fall. Investors, who had borrowed to buy stock, had to sell at a loss. The stock market plummeted. On 21 August the Ohio Life Insurance and Trust Company failed. Over-extended banks suspended specie payments. The October issue of Hunt's "Merchants' Magazine" reported, "The last month has witnessed one of the most disastrous financial revulsions which has [sic] visited the country for many years."[13] Americans quit buying foreign goods and customs duties, which were $63.9 million in fiscal year 1857, shrank to $41.8 million in fiscal year 1858. The nation was in the midst of the Panic of 1857.[14]

The sharp decline in revenue left the federal government with insufficient income to meet its obligations. By 1 July 1857, the public debt had risen to $28 million. Democratic Treasury Secretary Howell Cobb recommended raising the duties on imports. President James Buchanan, however, disagreed. In his annual message to Congress on 8 December 1857, he admitted the nation's financial problems. But, he did not believe the new tariff had had sufficient time to prove its benefits. He, therefore, recommended waiting before adjusting the tariff rates. The Democratically-controlled Congress, which had long espoused free-trade, agreed. Instead of raising tariff rates, Congress authorized the Treasury to issue $20 million in notes in December 1857 and to borrow another $20 million in June 1858. By October 1858 the public debt had reached nearly $45 million.[15]

In May 1858 Democratic House Speaker James L. Orr, of South Carolina, appointed Justin Morrill to the House Ways and Means Committee. He had already served on the Territories and Agricultural Committees. The appointment pleased Morrill and his constituents. He wrote Ruth, "At last I am promoted by the Speaker to a vacancy in the Committee of Ways and Means."[16] One voter expressed his gratitude for Morrill's new position, which might enable him to "influence legislation favorable" to his constituents, especially tariff rates on wool and woolens.[17] Over the next forty years Morrill would develop a reputation as Congress' most knowledgeable member on tariffs and wool's staunchest guardian.

On 6 December 1858, President Buchanan again addressed Congress. He reiterated the financial woes of the federal government, explaining the Treasury was having to borrow money to meet ordinary expenses. This time he urged Congress to raise the tariff rates, not only to provide additional income, but to increase manufacturers' confidence by affording some "incidental protection." Buchanan also recommended specific duties and characterized the ad valorem system as disadvantageous to the manufacturers.[18]

The House Ways and Means Committee responded with two bills. The first by John S. Phelps of Missouri would reinstate the 1846 rates until the economy righted itself. The second, by Justin Morrill, increased tariff rates for a long-term remedy and authorized a loan for immediate relief. Powerful southern members ensured that neither proposal passed. The country continued to struggle under the inadequate provisions of the 1857 Tariff.[19]

Throughout 1859 Morrill continued to work on a tariff bill. Advice, recommendations, and pleas poured in from special interests around the country. Vermont wool growers and manufacturers wanted a higher tariff on wool and woolens. Pennsylvania iron makers asked for increased rates on iron. One manufacturer sent a sheet of recommended rates on iron and wire. New York Republican leader Thurlow Weed asked Morrill to advise a New York company of the proposed rates on sugar, iron, lead and tin. Another individual suggested rates for hemp and copper. For every item covered in the tariff, at least one person must have written Morrill to plead their case.[20]

Henry Winter Davis of Maryland and William A. Howard of Michigan served with Morrill on the subcommittee charged with producing a new tariff. Both Davis and Howard deferred to Morrill. Although they offered advice, Morrill wrote the bill. Already people referred to it as the Morrill Tariff. In August 1859 Davis wrote Morrill, "I wish you all success in your hunt for new facts and methods for the improvement of *your* [emphasis added] bill. I fear I cannot add much to them but I will be only too glad to have the honor of doing battle for your work. It was rightly named: no one in the H. R. but you could have prepared it. . . ."[21]

The 1858 election, in which Morrill easily won reelection, had changed the makeup of Congress. When the Thirty-sixth Congress met in December 1859, the Senate remained under Democratic control, but the House had 113 Republicans, 93 administration Democrats, 8 anti-Lecompton Democrats, and 23 Southern Americans. The House easily elected William Pennington, a conservative New Jersey Republican, as speaker. Ohio Republican John Sherman became Chair of the Ways and Means Committee.[22]

Sherman considered Morrill "eminently fitted to prepare a tariff bill. He had been engaged in trade and commerce, was a man of sound judgment, perfectly impartial and honest."[23] On 12 March 1860, Morrill reported to the House a bill "to provide for the payment of outstanding Treasury Notes, to authorize a loan, to regulate and fix the duties on imports, and for other purposes." Southerners, seeking to obstruct the bill, objected to receiving the report. According to a House rule, any objection prevented a bill from reaching the floor. Sherman tried again the following day. Although a majority of members voted to suspend the impeding rule, the motion lacked the necessary two-thirds required to suspend. The House had to amend the rule before the Ways and Means Committee could report Morrill's bill. Even after Morrill reported the bill on 6 April opponents delayed debate for another week. During the delay, Morrill had one thousand copies of the bill printed for distribution to voters to win their support.[24]

Finally, on 13 April 1860, the debate began. On April 23 Morrill explained his bill to the House. He first proposed authorizing a $21 million loan to pay off the $20 million in short-term treasury notes. Interest on a long-term loan would be considerably cheaper than on the notes. Morrill then addressed the heart of the bill: a revision of the tariff. Present laws had not served the government's purposes. The public debt, $11 million in 1857, had increased to $59 million in 1859. To pay this and other debt contracted in 1842, the nation "ought to retrace our steps of extravagance." He believed the federal government "must pay as we go. . . . It is not fit that the Government of the United States should 'go to bed without its supper' every time the imports of the week fall short a million at the port of New York."[25] Only a complete tariff revision could pay the nation's debts and preserved the public credit.

Morrill considered financing the federal government by taxing imports a "certain evil" that contributed to the government's "from-hand-to-mouth" condition. Americans had to spend $100 million abroad to produce $15 million of revenue. Also, "non-discrimination and positive discrimination against our own people" had led to "over-trading" at a higher rate and for a longer period than ever before. In the previous ten years foreign imports had doubled and the trade-deficit had averaged over $40 million a year. "There must be something radically wrong in a system which produces these results." According to Morrill, the "something radically wrong" was the "transcendental philosophy" of free-trade. He considered the idea a "sunlit theory, rejected in practice by every civilized nation." Warning against a free-trade policy, Morrill called British free-trade and reciprocity "the most insidious scalping-knives we have to encounter." As long as duties on imports supported the government, free-trade was not possible.[26]

Seeking to allay southern fears, Morrill described his proposal as a revenue tariff, not a protective one. "There are no duties proposed on any article for the simple purpose of protection alone." Furthermore, he stressed, "The average rates of duty upon manufactured articles are not higher, but rather lower, than they are now." Also, he had attempted to treat agriculture, manufacturing, mining, and commerce fairly and equally. No one would "be made the beast of burden to carry the packs of others." This tariff would allow Americans to compete fairly with the rest of the world.[27]

While admitting he could not precisely predict the full effect of this tariff, Morrill felt confident it would produce $60 million a year income. Since income from land sales was unreliable, he wanted the government to keep expenses below $50 million a year. This would leave $4 million for interest on the public debt and $6 million for the principle. If the government followed this policy, it could pay off the debt within ten years.[28]

Although the president, the treasury secretary, many industrial leaders and members of both parties in Congress agreed in principle with Morrill's tariff bill, it still faced stiff opposition. Democrats Thomas Florence, of Pennsylvania, and Alabama's George Houstan led the resistance in the House. Florence offered a substitute bill that would revive the 1846 Tariff, but raise the rates and keep the ad valorem system. While Houstan assured the House, if given enough time, the 1857 Tariff would provide the needed income.[29]

Morrill refuted both arguments. The 1846 Tariff's ad valorem rates had led to such fraud that the United States' revenue laws were "almost equal in infamy" to those of Mexico and other countries whose laws were "a mere farce." The measures he proposed, Morrill said, would produce $60 million and the 1857 Tariff would not.[30]

In May 1860, Ways and Means Committee Chair John Sherman joined in the fight for Morrill's tariff bill. On May 7 he moved that debate over the bill stop the next day. After this motion passed, he rose to speak. The 1857 Tariff, according to Sherman, had proven to be "crude, ill-advised, and ill-digested." Congress had adopted it when prices were inflated and "the treasury overflowing." But conditions had changed drastically since 1857 and that tariff could not pay the ordinary expenses of the government. He explained Morrill had written the bill with the idea that taxes should do as "little injury" as possible to the country's industry and to "extend a reasonable protection" to "the great industries of agriculture, manufacture, and commerce." Sherman urged the House to pass the bill.[31]

Still, opponents and special interests amended the measure until it bore little resemblance to the original. Morrill then offered an amendment that would essentially restore the bill originally reported with some nonsubstantive modifications. Next Sherman proposed an amendment to the amendment that included almost all the original bill with minor modifications. This maneuver prevented any amendment to Sherman's amendment, except to add to it. House members apparently tired of the struggle and finally approved Morrill's tariff bill on 10 May 1860. The final vote was 105 to 64.[32]

But the bill had only overcome one hurdle and a much larger one awaited in the Senate. Democrats, including many powerful southerners, controlled the Senate and most opposed the measure. Also working against the bill, 1860 was an election year and the tariff was a contentious issue. In the Senate, Finance Committee Chair Robert M. T. Hunter of Virginia reported it, on 10 June, and immediately made a motion to postpone consideration until Congress' second session, after the elections. The Senate agreed to delay debate until December 1860.[33]

"Weary and worn with unending day and night labor on the Committee of Ways and Means,"[34] Morrill considered not running for reelection in 1860. Winter Davis pleaded with him to reconsider. Davis stressed the need for a new tariff bill and his belief that its passage depended on Morrill. Davis wrote, "There is no one who will prepare such a bill as well as yourself in the H. R. [House of Representatives] or who is likely to be there; for there is no one who has your experience and preparation and very few have your knowledge of the business of the country in detail."[35] As we know, Morrill accepted renomination and easily won reelection.

The Morrill Tariff, meanwhile, was having an impact even before it became law. Historian Sidney Ratner considered the increased duties on iron and wool the most significant direct changes proposed in the bill and speculated Morrill made them with the hope of winning Pennsylvania and some western states for the Republican party. With Democrats opposing any revision, Republicans naturally decided to make the tariff a campaign issue in the 1860 elections. The House had already passed the measure when Republicans met in Chicago for their national convention. The platform committee understood Pennsylvania, a traditional Democratic stronghold, was necessary for a Republican victory in the fall elections. The Pennsylvania delegation, including at least three "iron" men, demanded a strong protectionist statement. In an attempt to satisfy the Pennsylvania and New Jersey delegates, without offending Westerners, the platform committee wrote a compromise plank. It called for a revenue tariff with "such an adjustment of those imposts as to encourage the development of the industrial interests of the whole country."[36]

Abraham Lincoln, the Republican nominee in Chicago, like Morrill, had supported Henry Clay's "American System" with its protectionist policies. Party leaders heralded Republican support for a protective tariff in speeches throughout the summer, especially in Pennsylvania. Justin Morrill, suddenly a national figure, was in demand as a campaign speaker. A Republican National Committee Member, asking Morrill to speak in Pennsylvania, wrote, "Do go, your tariff record will help us. All must be done that can be."[37] Morrill and Sherman both toured Pennsylvania explaining the Republicans' protectionist policy to enthusiastic crowds. In an election with so many important issues, it is impossible to accurately assess the tariff's effect on the outcome. Historian Allan Nevins noted that Republican speakers supporting the Morrill bill were "effective in parts of the East, and particularly so in Pennsylvania." Congressman William McKinley, who later became president in 1896, believed that without the tariff issue Republicans would have lost Pennsylvania and the 1860 election. As it was, that state, which had voted Democratic in 1856, gave its 27 electoral votes to Lincoln.[38]

Lincoln's election prompted events that improved the measure's prospects of success. When the Senate reassembled in December, the senators from the seceded state of South Carolina had withdrawn. On 20 December, Hunter reported the tariff bill and recommended the Senate postpone consideration until 4 March 1861, the last day of the session.

Instead, the Senate referred the bill to a select committee. Before discussion on the tariff bill began, senators from Alabama, Florida, Georgia, Louisiana and Mississippi followed South Carolina's lead. On 23 January 1861, Pennsylvania Senator Simon Cameron moved that the Senate take up the bill. Rhode Island's James F. Simmons proposed appointing a new select committee to consider the measure. As part of the Senate's reorganization following the loss of twelve southern senators, the vice president appointed a new select committee of three Democrats: Hunter, Pennsylvania's William Bigler, and California's William M. Gwin, and two Republicans: Cameron and Maine's William P. Fessenden. Although Democrats outnumbered Republicans on the committee, Bigler favored the tariff bill.[39]

The select committee reported the bill favorably back to the Senate on 1 February 1861, but with many proposed amendments. Members debated the amendments, especially those on iron and wool. The present duty on wool was 24 percent on all valued at 20 cents or more a pound. The House would change that ad valorem rate to a specific rate of three cents a pound for wool valued at 18–23 cents a pound and nine cents a pound for that valued at 24 cents and above. The Senate added a 5 percent duty on wool valued below 18 cents a pound. After adding 156 amendments, the Senate passed the tariff bill on 20 February by a 25 to 14 vote, and returned it to the House. Obstructionists in the House insisted the body vote on each amendment separately. The House approved all amendments, except one that added a duty to coffee and tea. The Senate concurred and passed the bill on to the president. Buchanan signed Morrill's tariff bill into law on March 2 and it took effect on 1 April 1861.[40]

Southerners deplored the new tariff. Morrill later recalled that after the Civil War started a Virginia newspaper published his picture and offered $25 for Morrill dead or alive, the same reward as for a runaway slave. The article described him as "a person who would sooner be suspected to have been the author of Yankee Doodle than of the infernal tariff of 1861."[41] Morrill would leave it for posterity to determine if Vermonters had made a mistake in not surrendering him to collect the reward.

The Morrill Tariff also had an effect on foreign relations. Great Britain, the world's leading proponent of free-trade, resented the impediment to their commerce. On 15 March 1861, American historian John L. Motley wrote from London that although the English government regretted the threatened breakup of the United States, the Morrill Tariff had caused a shift in sympathy. According to Motley, "That measure has done more than any commissioner from the Southern republic could do to alienate the feelings of the English public towards the United States."[42]

Southern emissaries tried to exploit this resentment. They promised duty-free trade and a steady supply of cotton in their attempt to elicit British recognition of Confederate independence. The ploy did not work. Ultimately, British leaders decided they could best serve their nation's interests by being neutral and letting the Union and Confederate armies decide the war's outcome. But the tariff created friction between Washington and London throughout the war.[43]

On 12 April, eleven days after the Morrill Tariff became effective, Confederate forces opened fire on Fort Sumter, in Charleston's harbor. The Civil War had begun. When Congress reconvened in July 1861, the Union needed money to fight the war. On 16 July 1861, Thaddeus Stevens, Chair of the House Ways and Means Committee, reported a new tariff bill. It retained most of the Morrill Tariff's features, but added coffee and tea to the duty list and increased other rates, especially on luxury items. In December Congress increased the coffee, tea and sugar rates. The Tariff Act of 14 July 1862, which Allan Nevins called the Second Morrill Tariff, elevated duties again to protect American manufacturers from foreign competition and compensate for high internal taxes. Every session of Congress during the Civil War boosted tariff rates.[44]

Assessing the tariff in September 1865, Morrill felt that it had proven its worth. The only changes to the act, he said, were additions to increase revenue or to offset internal taxes. It did not halt imports, as some had feared, but "gave new life to all kinds of American Industry." He concluded, "It is hardly too much to say that the Tariff of 1861 and the maintenance of its principles sustained our armies in the field and that without it the people at home would have been subdued by idleness."[45]

After the war the Morrill Tariff and its protective tax sentiment continued to be part of Republican party platforms. Justification shifted, however, from protecting manufacturers to "securing remunerative wages to labor" or "promoting the interests of American labor." Since Republicans controlled at least one branch of the federal government until 1913, a protective tariff remained the national norm until then. Although Congress quickly reduced internal taxes after the Civil War, protectionists resisted decreases in the tariff. The 1872 Tariff yielded to public pressure and approved an across-the-board cut of 10 percent in duty rates. But Congress restored rates when a depression struck the following year. While the 1883 Tariff dropped rates on some articles, it raised duties on protected ones. The McKinley Tariff of 1890, the 1894 Wilson-Gorman Tariff, and the 1897 Dingley Tariff all maintained protective features. When Democratic President Grover Cleveland and the Democratically-controlled House tried to change this trend in 1888, the Republican-dominated Senate blocked passage of a free-trade tax reform bill. Protection remained in command until 1913, after Woodrow Wilson became president and the Democrats gained control over both houses of Congress.[46]

Despite its brief tenure, the Morrill Tariff had a lasting effect. First, it became a campaign issue, even before it passed, and helped elect Lincoln as president in 1860. With this bill, specific duties replaced most ad valorem rates. The Morrill Tariff also established a protectionist policy that lasted for over fifty years. Economic historian Sidney Ratner claimed Morrill reversed the tariff rates' downward trend and helped put and keep Republicans in power by winning the support of iron, cotton, woolen and other industrialists. James G. Blaine believed that Morrill had wrought a revolutionary change in the government's finances. But the tariff was not Morrill's only contribution to the Union cause during the war.[47]

Notes

1. William McKinley, *The Tariff; a review of the tariff legislation of the United States from 1812 to 1896* (New York: Putnam, 1904), 5.

2. F. W. Taussig, *The Tariff History of the United States* (New York: G. P. Putnam's Sons, 1931), 114–15; Davis Rich Dewey, *Financial History of the United States* (New York: Augustus M. Kelley Publishers, 1968), 262.

3. Morrill, speech, "On the Bill reported from the Committee of Ways and Means to reduce the Duties on Imports," delivered in the House of Representatives, 6 February 1857, LOC.

4. Ibid.

5. Ibid. Edward Stanwood, *American Tariff Controversies in the Nineteenth Century* (New York: Russell and Russell, 1904), 99–101.

6. Hoyer, "Gentleman from Vermont," 86–87; Stanwood, *American Tariff Controversies*, 101; Dewey, *Financial History*, 262–63.

7. Sidney Ratner, *The Tariff in American History* (New York: D. Van Nostrand Company, 1972), 10–23.

8. Robert Webster Welch, "Rhetorical Study of the Legislative Speaking of Congressman Justin Smith Morrill of Vermont in the U.S. House of Representatives on Selected Issues, 1855–1867" (Ph.D. diss., Pennsylvania State University, 1977), 30; J. Dewey to

Morrill, 9 February 1856, and D. Crawford to Morrill, 29 April 1856, LOC.

9. Welch, *Rhetorical Study*, 31.

10. Morrill to Edward Seymour, 9 April 1866, LOC.

11. Morrill to J. L. Laughlin, April 1883, LOC.

12. Dewey, *Financial History*, 264–65; Stanwood, *American Tariff Controversies*, 111–12; McKinley, *The Tariff*, 22–23.

13. Quoted in Stanwood, *American Tariff Controversies*, 114.

14. Ibid., 112–15; Dewey, *Financial History*, 264–65.

15. Stanwood, *American Tariff Controversies*, 115–19; Albert S. Bolles, *The Financial History of the United States, From 1789 to 1860* (New York: Augustus M. Kelley Publishers, 1969), 599–600.

16. Morrill to Ruth Morrill, quoted in Parker, *Morrill*, 93.

17. D. Crawford to Morrill, 5 January 1859, LOC.

18. Stanwood, *American Tariff Controversies*, 118–19.

19. Allan Nevins, *The Emergence of Lincoln* (New York: Charles Scribner's Sons, 1950), 1: 456–7.

20. D. Crawford to Morrill, 5 January 1859; John Kimball to Morrill, 12 January 1859; D. M. Daniel to Morrill, 12 January 1859; Thurlow Weed (telegram) to Morrill, 27 January 1859; Grinnell, Minturn and Co. to Morrill, 31 January 1859; I. M. Forbes to Morrill, 18 February 1859, LOC are a few examples.

21. Winter Davis to Morrill, 20 August 1859, LOC.

22. Stanwood, *American Tariff Controversies*, 119–20.

23. John Sherman, *Recollections of Forty Years in the House, Senate and Cabinet* (Chicago: Werner Company, 1895), 1: 183.

24. Parker, *Morrill*, 105–6; Stanwood, *American Tariff Controversies*, 120.

25. Morrill, speech, "The bill to provide for the payment of outstanding Treasury notes, to authorize a loan, to regulate and fix the duties on imports, and for other purposes," delivered in the House of Representatives, 23 April 1860, LOC.

26. Ibid.

27. Ibid.

28. Ibid.

29. Hoyer, "Gentleman from Vermont," 95.

30. Ibid.; Sherman, *Recollections*, 185–86.

31. Sherman, *Recollections*, 183–85.

32. Ibid., 186; Hoyer, "Gentleman from Vermont," 95–96; Parker, *Morrill*, 121.

33. Sherman, *Recollections*, 187; Stanwood, *American Tariff Controversies*, 122–23.

34. Parker, *Morrill*, 105.

35. Davis to Morrill, 1 August 1860, LOC.

36. Ratner, *Tariff in American History*, 29; Nevins, *Emergence of Lincoln*, 2: 253.

37. Wilson to Morrill, 25 September 1860, LOC.

38. Nevins, *Emergence of Lincoln*, 2: 304; Hoyer, "Gentleman from Vermont," 103–4.

39. Sherman, *Recollections*, 187; Stanwood, *American Tariff Controversies*, 122–3.

40. Sherman, Recollections, 187; Stanwood, *American Tariff Controversies*, 125–6; Parker, *Morrill*, 109–10.

41. Parker, *Morrill*, 111.

42. Ibid., 113.

43. Jay Monaghan, *Diplomat in Carpet Slippers: Abraham Lincoln Deals with Foreign Affairs* (Indianapolis: Bobbs-Merrill Company, 1945), 105; D. P. Crook, *The North, the South, and the Powers, 1861–1865* (New York: John Wiley and Sons, 1974), 21; Howard Jones, *The Union in Peril: The Crisis over British Intervention in the Civil War* (Chapel Hill: University of North Carolina Press, 1992), 34.

44. Stanwood, *American Tariff Controversies*, 126; Ratner, *Tariff in American History*, 29–30; Hoyer, "Gentleman from Vermont," 148; Allan Nevins, *War for the Union* (New York: Charles Scribner's Sons, 1960), 2: 490.

45. Morrill to J. E. Williams, 4 September 1865, LOC.

46. McKinley, *The Tariff*, 43, 48, 56, 67, 94; Ratner, *Tariff in American History*, 32–40.

47. Hoyer, ""Gentleman from Vermont,"" 100; Ratner, *Tariff in American History*, 112; James G. Blaine, *Twenty Years in Congress* (Norwich, Conn.: Henry Bill Company, 1884), 1: 278.

4

THE IRREPRESSIBLE CONFLICT

I regret the facts but we must accept the truth that there is an irrepressible conflict between our systems of civilizations.[1]

Justin Morrill, December 1860

The Civil War revolutionized the financial methods of the United States. A new monetary system was created, and tax resources before undreamed of were resorted to at first timorously, in the end with a rigor that hardly knew bounds.[2]

Historian F. W. Taussig

With Abraham Lincoln's election in 1860, southern states began calling conventions to consider secession. Although President Buchanan believed states could not legally secede, he also felt he could not legally stop them. Congress, meanwhile, sought another compromise to keep the nation from tearing apart. Justin Morrill reluctantly joined the House committee seeking a possible solution. When Congress failed and the war came, he devoted all his energy to raising money, through taxes and tariffs, to pay ordinary government expenses and interest and principle payments on the public debt. Without his efforts, Treasury Secretary Salmon Chase could never have borrowed the money needed to fight the war.

As the country prepared for the 1860 presidential election, southerners again threatened to leave the Union. Although the North and South had finally resolved the thorny Kansas question, another event had created an even greater rift between the two sections. On 16 October 1859, John Brown further divided the North and South when he and his "army" of twenty-two men attacked and captured the federal armory at Harper's Ferry, Virginia. Brown expected hundreds of slaves to rise up and join his band. Although no slaves revolted and Colonel Robert E. Lee and a company of Marines quickly overwhelmed Brown and his men, southerners saw Brown's raid as an attempt to instigate the long-feared slave insurrection. Letters, which authorities found in a nearby farmhouse linking Brown to several prominent northern supporters, were all the proof southerners needed that northerners had attempted to incite an armed slave revolt that would slaughter thousands of whites throughout the South. Widespread northern veneration of Brown following his execution convinced the South that the entire North, and especially the Republicans, condoned the plot.

By 1860 mutual distrust severely strained the bonds holding North and South together. The presidential election in November reflected the fragile state of the Union. Republicans nominated Abraham Lincoln on a platform denouncing disunionism, efforts to reopen the African slave trade, and the extension of slavery into the territories. The Republican platform also condemned John Brown's raid and promised to maintain each state's right to control its own "domestic institutions."

Democrats had a more difficult time, first with the platform, then with the candidate. Southerners demanded a platform affirming that neither Congress nor territorial government could deprive citizens of their constitutional right to take slaves into the territories. Northern delegates, who were in the majority, blocked the slave-code platform. Also, southerners refused to accept Stephen Douglas, the party's leading candidate, some preferring a Republican president to Douglas. Douglas supporters stood firm for his candidacy. After failing to agree on either candidate or platform, the Democrats split into two factions. Douglas became the candidate for the northern Democrats on a platform endorsing popular sovereignty and obedience to the Supreme Court decision on the territories. The southern Democrats nominated Vice President John Breckinridge as their standard-bearer and adopted their slave-code platform.[3]

To further separate the voters, a group of "opposition" members of Congress, Whigs, and American Party representatives held their own convention. This Constitutional Union Party adopted no platform but vowed to stand on the Constitution and the Union. Their candidate, John Bell of Tennessee, was a life-long Whig and a large slaveholder.

Throughout the campaign, southerners promised to secede if the Republican candidate became president. Northerners considered the threats as more southern blustering to win concessions on slavery. Southern opposition to the "black" Republicans was so strong that Lincoln did not appear on any ballot in the South. On 6 November, 1.8 million free state voters supported Lincoln. His combined opponents received 2.8 million votes. But Lincoln won 180 electoral votes, 27 more than he needed to become president. Douglas ran second with nearly a million votes, but he captured only one state. Breckinridge with less than 700 thousand votes carried eleven southern states. Bell with under 600 thousand votes won Virginia, Kentucky, and Tennessee's electoral votes. For the first time a candidate with no support in nearly half of the country became president. The nation was truly divided.[4]

In the winter of 1860–61, following the election, congressional leaders tried to find some compromise that would avert the threatened war. The Senate created a Committee of Thirteen and the House a Committee of Thirty-three (one from each state) to seek an understanding that might yet save the country. House Speaker William Pennington named Morrill to represent Vermont. Morrill had voted for the committee, but doubted the Union could be saved. Sixteen congressmen, including two committee members, had refused to vote because their states had called secession conventions. Morrill unsuccessfully tried to persuade retiring Congressman Stephen Royce to take his place. He felt certain there would "be no compromise short of an entire surrender of our convictions of right and wrong, and I do not propose to make that surrender."[5]

The Committee of Thirty-three met daily, but could find no common ground. Morrill wrote Ruth, "The weather here is gloomy and the times are gloomy." The slave states asked "for new guarantees for Slavery. We can only give the old ones." He felt "[d]isappointed men and the chronic disease in South Carolina" were behind the threatened breakup. But they gained courage from President Buchanan's weakness "or worse." Morrill acknowledged the times were "big with the fate of nations and surely try men's souls. . . . I do not think the secession Cholera will leave a single slave state untouched."[6]

Despite his certainty that nothing would come of the committee's efforts, Morrill and others searched for an answer they did not expect to find. Republican members seemed ready to compromise. They made several radical proposals, including compensation for fugitive slaves, allowing states to decide slavery through popular sovereignty, and immediate admission of all territories to statehood. Indiana Republican McKee Dunn offered a resolution supporting "any reasonable, proper, and constitutional" remedy that would guarantee the South's "peculiar rights and interests as recognized by the Constitution." Morrill offered a milder substitute measure, but the committee accepted Dunn's.[7]

Southerners, however, suspected the Republicans lacked sincerity in their compromise efforts. Mississippi Democrat Reuben Davis accused them of making promises they had no intention of keeping. On 14 December, the night after the Committee of Thirty-three approved Dunn's resolution, thirty southern senators and congressmen issued a manifesto stating, "The argument is exhausted. All hope of relief in the Union through the agencies of committees, congressional legislation, or constitutional amendments is extinguished, and we trust the South will not be deceived by appearances or the pretense of new guarantees."[8]

Though the situation seemed hopeless, the committee worked on. Orris S. Ferry of Connecticut proposed strengthening the Constitution to allow slave-owners to carry their "property" to the territories. William Kellogg of Illinois suggested setting up territorial governments with "authority over all subjects not inconsistent with the Constitution of the United States." Maryland Democrat Henry Winter Davis, who had considerable Republican support, introduced a resolution for Congress to urge states to repeal all laws that interfered with enforcement of the Fugitive Slave Law. The committee accepted Davis' resolution without debate. Republicans were flexible on the recovery of fugitive slaves. But despite Ferry and Kellogg's proposals, their party would not compromise on slavery's expansion into the territories.[9]

While Republicans vainly looked for a solution, Morrill believed northern Democrats had abandon all effort to save the Union. In frustration he wrote, "Caleb Cushing and Mayor [Fernando] Wood of N.Y. deserve to be hung before we stretch the necks of anybody in South Carolina." By late January 1861, Morrill was so discouraged he doubted the states would ever be united again.[10]

The Republican committee members apparently agreed they could do nothing to placate the cotton states. So they developed a strategy to divide the lower South and the Border States, including Virginia. Henry Winter Davis had suggested admitting New Mexico (a slave state) and Kansas (a free state) to the Union. Republicans supported the admission of New Mexico, without mentioning Kansas. They had consulted with Judge John S. Watts, who had spent nine years in New Mexico, and realized conditions there were not conducive to slavery. This proposal allowed the Republicans to maintain their stand against the extension of slavery into the territories and avoid any promise of future slave states. Another Republican resolution guaranteed against federal interference with slavery within the states.[11]

Charles Francis Adams sponsored these resolutions, although he did not write them. The committee first voted on the measure to protect slavery in the states. Members agreed 21 to 3. Morrill supported the resolution, but with a heavy heart. He wrote Ruth, "I felt it to be my duty to vote for it but no vote I ever gave has caused me so much severe thought." But he was sure his sacrifice would be in vain.[12]

The second proposal on admitting New Mexico into the Union also passed. The vote was 13 to 11, with Morrill voting in opposition. Asking him to admit another slave state, even a nominal one, was asking too much. But two Border State members voted for it and all other slave state members abstained or opposed the measure. Adams' son Henry claimed this vote divided the slave-state coalition. Although this is probably an overstatement, it did drive at least a small wedge between them. The senior Adams then introduced a resolution stating every good citizen had a duty to peacefully acquiesce in the election of a president. The measure passed 22 to 0, with Virginia, Kentucky, Tennessee and Maryland's representatives voting for it and seven cotton state members abstaining. The Republican strategy apparently succeeded.[13]

Little else came from the committee's efforts. Although the Committee of Thirty-three had approved resolutions to admit New Mexico and amend the Constitution to protect slavery in the states, only six members voted to ask the full House to concur with these proposals. Morrill opposed the motion. In the last session before Congress adjourned on 2 March 1861, the House accepted only the resolution to amend the Constitution. But the states never approved it.[14]

Morrill stayed in Washington for Abraham Lincoln's inauguration on 4 March. He considered the event the "most magnificent one we have ever had." Lincoln's address displayed "extraordinary tact. Conciliatory but firm." Even as Morrill prepared to leave Washington for Vermont, he expected to return soon. Southern members had thwarted attempts to pass bills to pay normal government debts, so he anticipated the president's calling a special session to address the problem.[15]

President Lincoln, however, waited until 4 July 1861, before calling Congress into special session. He had been content to deal with the rebelling states for four months without congressional interference. Lincoln had proclaimed a blockade of southern ports, increased the size of the Army and Navy, extended volunteer enlistments to three years, authorized private citizens to spend public funds to purchase arms and supplies, and suspended the writ of habeas corpus. In his July 4 message to Congress the president explained, "These measures, whether strictly legal or not, were ventured upon, under what appeared to be a popular demand, and a public necessity; trusting, then, as now, that Congress would readily ratify them." Lincoln also recommended that Congress allocate $400 million to support a 400 thousand-man army. Congress hesitated to approve all Lincoln's extraordinary measures, but immediately responded by appropriating $500 million for an army of 500 thousand men.[16]

Even before this grand congressional gesture, federal finances were in disarray. According to John Sherman, Howell Cobb, the previous treasury secretary, "had aided in every possible way to cripple the department" before his "duty to Georgia" forced him to resign on 10 December 1860. The Treasury was so empty there was no money to pay congressional salaries in December 1860. The public debt had risen to $75 million by March 1961 when the Republicans assumed control. Salmon Chase, the new treasury secretary, had to rely on previous loan acts to provide income until Congress met.[17]

With the southern withdrawal, Republicans dominated the second session of the 37th Congress. Justin Morrill became the ranking member of the Ways and Means Committee. But he deferred to Thaddeus Stevens, who was nearly twenty years older and had first served in Congress in 1849. Morrill explained to Ruth, "I could have the Chairmanship of the Ways and Means, but I have declined it. The work is very great and I dursn't undertake it."[18]

Stevens separated Ways and Means into three subcommittees. He accepted responsibility for appropriations. Elbridge G. Spaulding of New York chaired a committee to handle loans. Stevens recognized Morrill's tariff expertise and named him to head the war tax program. Secretary Chase, like most people in the federal government, did not expect a long war. So he asked for a $240 million loan to finance the war and $80 million in taxes to pay ordinary expense, interest on the loan, and create a sinking fund to pay off the public debt. The secretary suggested raising the $80 million by increasing tariff duties, a direct tax of $20 million apportioned among the states according to population, and a tax on alcoholic beverages, tobacco, bank notes, and other domestic articles.[19]

On July 16 Stevens reported a new tariff bill, which was basically the same as the Morrill Tariff with provisions to increase the revenue.[20] The bill proposed a general increase in rates, with a large jump in duties on liquor, wine, sugar and cigars. Coffee and tea, which were duty-free, would be taxable. Clement L. Vallandigham, the southern-sympathizing Democrat from Ohio, led the opposition to the bill. Morrill spoke in its defense, although he believed Stevens had overestimated income from the bill. He warned that other measures, including a direct tax and an income tax, would be necessary to meet the war's huge expenditures. Stevens called for a vote on July 18. The House quickly passed the bill by an 82 to 48 vote and sent it on to the Senate.[21]

Just three days later, on 21 July, the Confederate victory at Bull Run awakened Congress and the nation to the prospect of a prolonged conflict. Moving quickly Stevens, on 24 July, reported the internal revenue bill that Morrill had written, which included a direct tax on real estate and an excise tax on personal property, including watches, carriages, horses, bank notes, etc. Speaking for the bill, Morrill noted that Vermont opposed a direct tax, but emphasized the Treasury's dire condition. Although loans were to sustain the war effort, the bonds would not sell without a tax bill to guarantee interest payments. He concluded his remarks by asking, "Do we sustain the war effort or not?"[22]

Despite the obvious need and Morrill and Stevens' arguments, representatives opposed a $30 million direct tax. Illinois Congressman John McClernand suggested cutting the tax in half. Stevens resisted any reduction. Morrill interceded and suggested a $20 million direct tax. McClernand agreed and the bill returned to the Ways and Means Committee for changes. The modified bill incorporated the $20 million direct tax and added a 3 percent tax on all incomes above $600 a year. Western members resisted the direct tax, complaining the tax would hit western states hardest because most of their wealth was in land. Morrill explained the direct tax would fall heavier on individual western farmers, but the income tax would most affect eastern manufacturers. He added that he expected the income tax to raise twice as much as the direct tax.[23]

The Senate passed amended versions of both the tariff and the internal tax bills. Both went to a joint conference committee, which combined them into a so-called tariff bill. The compromise reduced the coffee duty from five to four cents, raised the lower income tax limit from $600 to

$800, and eliminated the excise taxes. The new tariff rates would be effective immediately. The income tax was delayed until 1 January 1862 and the direct tax until 1 April 1862. Both Houses passed the much-modified measure on 2 August, the House by a 77 to 60 margin and the Senate by 34 to 8. President Lincoln signed it on 5 August 1861.[24]

The direct tax was a one-time assessment. While its backers expect the measure to provide quick relief, proceeds were sporadic and sometimes nonexistent. The tax upon real estate applied to all states, even those in rebellion. Apportioned according to population, the assessment was largest in the populous industrial states. New York's portion was $2,603,918.66. Pennsylvania owed $1,946,719.33. In the west, California was to pay $254,538.66 and Oregon $35,140.66. In 1874 northern states still owed about $1.5 million on the direct tax. The rebel states' assessment was $5,153,891.33, which they, of course, did not pay. After the war, tax commissioners seized and sold an estimated $700,000 worth of land in former Confederate states to satisfy part of the direct tax assessment.[25]

On 5 August Congress passed another "revenue" act authorizing the confiscation of all property used to aid or support the Confederate cause. Since "property" included slaves, this bill touched off excited debate in both Houses of Congress. Border State members, led by Kentucky's John J. Crittenden, argued that since Congress had no power to control slavery in the states, it also lacked the authority to confiscate slaves used in the rebellion. Illinois' William Kellogg countered Congress could punish treason by taking the traitor's house, land and property. The penalty would operate against the individual, not against the institution. Republican Senator Henry Lane of Indiana spoke for many when he said, "[A]lthough the abolition of slavery is not an object of the war, they [southerners] may, in their madness and folly and treason, make the abolition of slavery one of the results of the war."[26]

When the special session of Congress ended on 6 August 1861, Justin Morrill was happy to return to Strafford. He had worked hard on the appropriation bills and Washington summers sapped his strength. He deserved and needed a respite before the next session of Congress convened on 2 December.[27]

But while Morrill tended to personal business, the nation's finances were in crisis. There was simply not enough "hard" money available to conduct the government's business. Secretary Chase estimated that $210 million in coin was circulating, including the cash in banks. This amount was sufficient for the prewar economy, but not enough for wartime. In the summer and fall of 1861, Chase negotiated three $50 million loans from American banks. According to conditions Congress imposed in the July loan act, the federal government paid creditors in bank notes, which the banks had to redeem in coin or "specie." As war expenses mounted, bankers warned Chase they could not continue to redeem in hard currency. He, however, was not ready to recommend the government issue notes designated as legal tender.[28]

The week after Congress reconvened, Chase submitted his report on the nation's finances on 9 December. He cheerfully reported good progress on the loans, having borrowed nearly $200 million: $146 million in advances from New York, Philadelphia and Boston banks, and $51 million in Treasury notes. About half these Treasury notes bore no interest, were payable on demand, and circulated as money. Chase explained that federal income, however, estimated at $80 million in July, would be closer to $55 million. He attributed this difference to Congress' reluctance to adopt the duty rates he had recommended and to strained American-British relations, following the *Trent Affair*, that hampered trade.[29] Also, expenses would far exceed earlier estimates, since Congress had authorized 500 thousand troops instead of the 400 thousand asked for. Chase sought an additional $213 million.[30]

To raise the extra money, the secretary recommended reducing expenses, closely scrutinizing all federal contracts, abolishing unneeded offices, lowering federal salaries, and forfeiting rebel property. He would also increase tariff duties on sugar, tea and coffee. The direct tax, he believed, should be set at $20 million annually. Also, internal taxes on stills, liquor, tobacco, banknotes, carriages, deeds, and other personal property could raise another $20 million. Chase further proposed modifying the income tax to add another $10 million. Loans would make up the $163 million difference.[31]

Just three weeks after Chase's encouraging report on the progress of the loans, the nation's banks suspended specie payments on 28 December. The Treasury notes Chase had issued were not being redeemed in coin on demand. Banks would no longer accept the notes as payment on account and they had almost stopped circulating. Bankers explained the government's demand that the banks advance the $146 million, instead of allowing them to keep it until it was actually needed, and the obligation to redeem Treasury notes in coin was a burden too heavy to carry.[32]

E. G. Spaulding, Morrill's colleague on Ways and Means, quickly responded to the crisis. He added a section to a banking bill, then in committee, authorizing the Treasury to issue $150 million in legal tender notes. These Treasury notes would be valid for payment of "all debts, public or private." After realizing the banking bill might take months to pass, Spaulding detached the legal tender section and submitted it as a separate bill on 30 December. Congress suspended specie payment on 31 December.[33]

Morrill, ever a fiscal conservative, strongly opposed the measure, though Spaulding was a fellow Republican serving on the Ways and Means Committee with him. On 4 February 1862, Morrill spoke against the "Impolicy of making Paper Money a Legal Tender." He acknowledged the patriotism of the bill's authors and supporters, but questioned the wisdom of their measure. This bill would damage the country's credit, prevent borrowing, inflate the currency, increase the cost of the war, and lead to a premature peace agreement. He also questioned the constitutionality of issuing paper money as legal tender. Paper money, Morrill argued, would undermine people's confidence in the government and thwart efforts to borrow money needed to conduct the war. He believed people would remove their currency from circulation and hoard it. Morrill warned that once paper money became legal tender "we shall sever all connections with any other fountains of supply." Then there could be not turning back, "we cannot retrace our steps, but must go on. . . . I would as soon provide Chinese wooden guns for the Army as paper money alone for the Treasury," he proclaimed. He passionately closed his argument saying "With all the earnestness I possess I do protest against making anything legal tender but gold and silver, as calculated to undermine all confidence in that Republic whose reputation should be dearer to statesmen . . . than life itself."[34]

Instead, Morrill proposed allowing the $50 million in Treasury notes to continue to circulate and guaranteeing their redemption in coin. Also, the Treasury should issue $200 million in ten-year and $300 million in twenty-five-year bonds, with interest payable semiannually in coin. This substitute, he claimed, would relieve the Treasury's current problems and provide for future need.[35]

Spaulding countered Morrill's arguments with a letter from Secretary Chase urging the bill's passage. Supporters also explained the government must pay $350 million before July 1862, $100 million of which was already due to soldiers and other creditors. Thaddeus Stevens, in the

House, and John Sherman, in the Senate, added their weight to the bill's support. The House passed the bill, on 6 February, by a 93 to 59 margin. Morrill and a few fellow Republicans joined the Democrats in opposition. The Senate approved the Legal Tender Act a week later by a 30 to 7 vote. After a conference committee compromised on differences and both Houses accepted the amended version, President Lincoln signed the bill on 25 February 1862.[36]

Debate had hardly ended on the Legal Tender Act when Morrill presented another internal tax bill on 12 March 1862. In a speech to the House, he explained this bill had "its fingers spread in all directions, ready to clutch something to buoy up the sinking credit of a nation which [had] hitherto generally sheltered its capital and its labor from all tax gatherers," except customs duties. The bill included: a 3 percent ad valorem tax on all manufactured goods, which Morrill estimated would raise $50 million, a large increase in tobacco and alcoholic beverage taxes, which should bring in another $24 million, and a higher income tax rate. Commenting on the tax on whiskey, Morrill said even with the duty added it would still be possible "for any man or brute to get drunk in our land on cheaper terms than in any other I know of." The 1861 tax bill had established a 3 percent rate on all incomes over $800 a year. Morrill proposed a 3 percent rate on incomes between $600 and $10 thousand and 5 percent (later changed to 10 percent) on incomes above $10 thousand.[37]

To ensure the proposed tax money flowed to the Treasury, the bill would create an internal revenue department responsible directly to the treasury secretary. Each state would have a collector, an assessor, and as many deputies as necessary. This last section caused the most opposition to the bill. California Congressman Timothy G. Phelps suggested eliminating the assessors to save money. Morrill countered that the need for checks and balances and the volume of work justified both positions. A Massachusetts representative suggested saving the cost of salaries by letting the states collect the money. But Morrill argued, if the states faltered, the delays and problems in collecting would more than offset any savings.[38]

Stevens then assumed responsibility for the bill, allowing Morrill time to write another tariff revision. On 8 April Stevens closed debate with a short speech supporting the measure. The House approved the bill 125 to 14. The Senate spent the next two months arguing and amending. Finally, the Upper House approved the measure on 6 June by a 37 to 1 margin and returned it to the House with 312 amendments. The House, under Stevens' directions and with Morrill's concurrence, rejected the amendments en masse. In the joint conference, however, Stevens accepted nearly all the amendments, explaining he had acted to spare the House the tedium of discussing each amendment. The changes altered the bill's details, but not its substance. Congressman James Blaine later recalled:

> The butcher paid thirty cents for every beef slaughtered, ten cents for every hog, five cents for every sheep. . . . Every profession and every calling, except the ministry of religion, was included within the far-reaching provisions of the law and subjected to tax for license. Bankers and pawnbrokers, lawyers and horse-dealers, physicians and confectioners, commercial brokers and peddlers, proprietors of theatres and jugglers on the street, were indiscriminately summoned to aid the National Treasury.[39]

Both Houses accepted the new version of the measure and President Lincoln endorsed it on 1 July 1862.[40]

Congress then shifted its focus to the next tariff bill. Both Morrill and Stevens believed the heavy internal taxes on domestic producers gave foreign manufacturers an unfair advantage in the American market. In presenting his tariff revision, Morrill explained it would "increase the revenue upon importations from abroad, and, at the same time, shelter and nurse our domestic products." Western Democrats argued higher duties would place an unfair burden on agriculture in their states. Since the bill required payment in specie, they felt it would transfer the western farmers' wealth to eastern industrialists. Morrill countered, "If we bleed the manufacturer, we must see to it that the proper tonic is administered at the same time."[41]

President Lincoln signed this second Morrill Tariff into law on 14 July 1862. The new measure included a compound duty on wool, with a graduated tax on raw wool and an ad valorem duty on manufactured products. Duties on drugs and products containing alcohol increased. Generally, steel and iron rates equaled the internal tax. The rates on silks were significantly higher. The new rates were often so high they effectively kept foreign products from entering the country. Increased rates and great wartime demands were a boon to America's iron industry. Iron men renovated old factories and built new ones. Several states benefited, but Pennsylvania experienced a boom. New rolling mills in Allentown and Bethlehem produced 40 thousand tons annually. Another rolling mill opened in Sharon and two steel mills in Pittsburgh. Pennsylvania's railroad industry also thrived. The tariff was obviously the "proper tonic" for that state.[42]

Although Congress had raise tariff and internal tax rates, expenses continued to grow at a much faster pace than income. In the first six months of 1862 loans did not make up the difference. Secretary Chase issued legal tender notes (or "greenbacks" as they quickly became known) to meet expenses. But by June he had already reached the limit set in the February law. In a 7 June 1862 letter to House Ways and Means Chair Stevens, Chase explained the situation. Congress has authorized the issuance of $150 million in legal tender notes, but earmarked $60 million of that sum to replace older demand notes. The Treasury had already issued the $90 million difference. Because of pressing obligations and lagging resources, Chase asked that Congress authorize him to issue another $150 million in greenbacks.

Morrill again opposed the idea. He had predicted in February, during the debate on the first Legal Tender Act, "Within sixty days we must have at least twice the amount of notes that is proposed now."[43] Although the request came after 120 days, this did not soften his position. With recent Union victories and the passing of the tax bill, Morrill saw no necessity or any excuse for issuing more paper money. Circulating more legal tender notes was a breach of faith to the banks that had bought bonds, he declared. He believed greenbacks were inherently worthless and undermined the war finance program. Instead, he suggested selling government bonds at whatever price they would bring. Despite Morrill's opposition, Stevens backed the measure and the House approved the second Legal Tender Act on 24 June 1862 by a 76 to 47 vote. President Lincoln signed the bill authorizing the Secretary of the Treasury to issue another $150 million in United States notes.[44]

Meanwhile, as the war dragged on, casualties mounted among Vermont's troops. Morrill often visited nearby hospitals and offered encouragement to his fellow Vermonters. In April 1862 he learned that Vermont forces had suffered heavy casualties at Yorktown, Virginia. A civilian witness told Morrill the general commanding the Union forces during the battle was so drunk he had fallen off his horse twice. The news so outraged Morrill that he offered a resolution, which the House approved, requesting the president to "strike from the rolls" the name of those "habitually intoxicated" while in service.[45]

After this grueling session, Morrill returned to Strafford to rest. Although he worked harder than almost anyone else in Congress, he was prone to illness and, therefore, needed to guard his health. The heat and disease of Washington summers taxed his strength. The constant pressure of supplying money to fight the Civil War also took a toll on him. In Vermont, he could relax and recover his vitality. He usually spent his summers reading, visiting with family and friends, and making personal business trips to Boston and New York.[46]

As Morrill mentioned in his speech opposing the second Legal Tender Act, the Union had achieved several victories in the first half of 1862. The North had won battles at Pea Ridge, Fort Donelson, Fort Henry, Shiloh, and had taken New Orleans. General George McClellan and his mighty Army of the Potomac were poised to seize Richmond. In late June, however, Robert E. Lee's boldness and McClellan's tendency to overestimate his opponent's numbers allowed a smaller Confederate Army to roust the Union Army and force it to retreat. With Lee's victory in this Seven-Days Campaign, the tide of battle shifted to favor the South. Although McClellan stopped Lee's advance into Maryland in September 1862, the lack of northern victories and rumors that England would soon recognize the Confederacy wiped away the optimism of earlier months.

When Congress met on 1 December 1862, conditions seemed bleak. The Treasury faced a $276 million deficit, including nearly $29 million in unpaid Army requisitions. Hundreds of thousands of additional troops greatly increased the cost of the war. Inflation consumed much of the available revenue. Additionally, there was a lack of circulating currency. To offer immediate relief for the Army's unpaid requisitions, Stevens introduced a resolution authorizing the Treasury to issue $50 million in greenbacks. Owen Lovejoy, of Illinois, made the motion to increase the amount to $100 million. Both Houses approved the resolution and President Lincoln signed it on 17 January 1863.[47]

On 12 January 1863, Stevens reported a "Ways and Means" bill authorizing the sale of $900 million in bonds, $300 million in interest-bearing treasury notes, and the issuance of $300 million in non-interest-bearing demand notes (greenbacks). Although Stevens reported the bill, he opposed the $300 million in interest-bearing notes' section. Spaulding responded that the nation must realize the great cost of fighting the war and the entire bill was necessary. Spaulding received help from a surprising source. On January 13 Justin Morrill spoke supporting the bill even though it would authorize another $300 million in greenbacks. Clarifying his position, he explained:

I abate not a jot of my repugnance to a legislative attempt—not yet successful—to make even gilt-edged paper a universal solvent or measure of value, instead of gold and silver, and it is not my will that consents, but the poverty of the Treasury that compels me to follow the only path left open. . . The patient has got accustomed to opiates and the dose cannot be withheld without peril. . . . If we cannot obtain a foundation of rock, let us, at least, dig for hard-pan.[48]

He expected $900 million would finance the war for a year and a half. If the war lasted longer, then more money would be needed. But, he stressed, liberty and Union were worth any price. He admitted military successes were important to the nation's financial health, but public support and faith also played a significant role. According to Morrill biographer William Parker, Morrill changed his position after Chase threatened to resign, if the measure did not pass, and support Morrill as his replacement as treasury secretary. In either case, the Ways and Means bill finally became law on 3 March 1863.[49]

The day after President Lincoln signed the bill into law, Congress adjourned. This allowed Morrill to return to Strafford's restorative climate. He and his family took a leisurely trip to St. Paul, Minnesota. Meanwhile, Vermont had postponed its 1862 election until 1 September 1863. In keeping with his desire to stay at home and tend to his personal business, Morrill had decided to retire and not seek reelection. He told his House colleague Schuyler Colfax:

> You know my health is not robust—and my business, of less importance, has had little attention for years, while my home is broken in fragmentary parts. I do not love office nor do I feel able to win any permanent reputation. I merely desire to live and die a quiet and honest citizen—wronging no friend and an ardent lover of his country.[50]

His constituents, however, would not accede to his retirement. Instead they drafted and reelected him to the House for his fifth term.[51]

When Congress convened on 7 December 1863, conditions were much improved from the previous year. Secretary Chase reported income for the 1863 fiscal year was $124 million plus $590 million from loans. This covered the $714 million in expenditures. The national debt, as of 1 July 1863, amounted to $1.01 billion. Union victories at Vicksburg and Gettysburg had significantly improved morale and confidence in the administration and eventual northern success. Chase estimated war costs for the 1864 fiscal year would be $755 million. Income of $161.5 million and $594 million in loans would meet these expenses.[52]

Unfortunately, rising prices and a devalued dollar made Chase's predictions too optimistic. Morrill reported another Internal Revenue Bill on 19 April 1864. The size and length of the war had far exceeded his expectations. Although the cost was unprecedented, he reminded his constituents the Union's resources were "equal to all emergencies, and to any campaign. . . . Let us have taxes, let us have loans; something, at all events, which will reduce the amount of legal-tenders now outstanding, and increase the value of the pay of the soldier."[53] Morrill, therefore, proposed increasing the tax on manufactured goods and incomes from 3 to 5 percent and income from securities from 1 1/2 to 2 1/2 percent. Rates on tobacco, alcohol, railroads and iron would be higher. He also proposed new taxes on gold and silver products and the gross receipts of theaters, operas, circuses and museums. Morrill estimated the income from this bill would be $250 million a year, enough to cover annual expenses of $100 million and interest on a $3 billion debt. Congress approved the measure and President Lincoln signed it on 30 June 1864.[54]

Even before the internal revenue bill passed Congress, Morrill proposed a corresponding tariff increase. On June 2 he explained to the House the tariff also needed to produce additional income to compensate for the high war costs. The higher tariff also would allow home industries paying more internal taxes to compete with imported goods. The greatest increases were on alcohol, tobacco and luxury items. Necessities, such as sugar, experienced smaller boosts. He admitted the rates were far higher than usual to protect domestic industry, but denied they were prohibitive. Both the House and Senate quickly passed Morrill's tariff bill and Lincoln also endorsed it on June 30. Surprisingly, these extremely high tariff rates stayed in effect for the next twenty years.[55]

In the midst of Morrill's efforts to raise more revenue, he saw an opportunity to rid Vermont and the nation of what he considered a drain on national resources: the reciprocity treaty with Canada. The United States and Great Britain had signed the treaty governing trade between the U.S. and Canada on 5 June 1854. Besides granting mutual fishing rights in territorial waters, the treaty listed agricultural products and raw materials the two countries would admit duty-free. Because of its proximity, Vermont considered Canada a rival for local markets and opposed the treaty even before it reached the Senate. In 1852 the state legislature passed a resolution against such a treaty. Initially, Americans in other states reacted favorably to reciprocity. But, when the nation suffered an economic depression in 1857, many people complained the treaty contributed to their woes.[56]

As American economic pressures grew during the Civil War, the cry for abrogation of the treaty became louder. People complained the treaty did not cover manufactured goods and Canada imposed high tariffs on these products. Also, the local Canadian government looked the other way as Confederate agents used Canada as a base for raids against northern states. So, not surprisingly, Justin Morrill conducted a campaign to end the treaty. Although neither side could terminate the agreement before 1866, in 1858 he asked for a resolution to investigate treaty operations. In an 1860 tariff speech he claimed reciprocity had been disastrous for the United States. In March 1860 the House passed a resolution asking the president to provide all the information in his possession on the working of the treaty.[57]

On 27 January 1864, Morrill proposed a joint resolution ending the treaty. He cited three reasons for repeal. First, it violated the Constitution by depriving the House of Representatives of the right to regulate commerce and levy and collect duties. Second, under the treaty, Canadian exports to the United States had increased, while American exports to Canada had declined. Finally, Morrill noted an original purpose of reciprocity had been to improve relations with Canada, with the hope of annexing that country to the United States. But, under the treaty, American-Canadian relations had deteriorated. In a later report he claimed the treaty had destroyed a $15 million-a-year trade between northeastern cities and Canada.[58]

After considerable debate in both Houses, Congress approved a joint resolution proposing an unconditional abrogation of the treaty, "as it is no longer for the interests of the United States to continue the same in force." President Lincoln approved the resolution on 18 January 1865. The treaty ended 17 March 1866. In subsequent years, Morrill fought against reciprocity treaties with Cuba, Mexico and Hawaii, and again with Canada. In 1887 he explained to the secretary of the Philadelphia Board of Trade:

I am utterly opposed to any commercial union with Canada or any Reciprocity Treaty. No arrangement could be made that would not leave us with a loss of more than five to one. [The previous treaty] tended to sap and mine a protective tariff, robbed us from the benefit of our neighbors-in-law, and all done in palpable violation of our Constitution.[59]

To help offset the weariness of his struggle against the treaty and the constant effort to raise more money, Morrill brought his family to Washington for the long 1864 session. Ruth used the opportunity to solicit funds for the Ladies Relief Society for Soldiers. Six-year-old Jimmy spent many hours playing on the floor of the House of Representatives. Thaddeus Stevens especially liked Jimmy and dubbed him "Little Ways and Means." "Uncle" Thaddeus delighted in raising Jimmy's hand to vote on official matters.[60]

Meanwhile, on 30 June 1864, Salmon Chase resigned as treasury secretary and President Lincoln appointed Senate Finance Committee Chair William Pitt Fessenden to the position. When Congress reconvened on 5 December, Fessenden reported the Treasury had only $19 million on hand, with $72 million in unpaid requisitions and $169 million due on certificates of indebtedness. In February 1865 Morrill introduced his last wartime tax bill. Most taxes increased from 5 to 6 percent, but this time the whiskey tax stayed the same. Meanwhile, Morrill proposed to revise the tariff schedule. Instead of a general rate increase, the bill would add an ad valorem duty to the current specific rates. Both measures quickly passed Congress and the president signed them on 3 March 1865. On 9 April 1865 General Lee surrendered his Army of Northern Virginia and the Civil War was essentially over. Six days later President Lincoln died and Andrew Johnson became president.[61]

Although Morrill was slow to realize the war would not end quickly, the tax and tariff measures he wrote provided substantial income and made the loan program possible. Total revenue grew from approximately $52 million in 1862[62] to nearly $560 million in 1866. Although expenditures far outstripped income during the war years, rising from $565 million in 1862 to almost $2 billion in 1865, the federal government was able to borrow enough to make-up the difference. Without the revenue he helped generate to pay interest and repay the loans, the treasury secretary could not have borrowed the money to fight the war. Despite the heavy burden of tax and tariff legislation during the Civil War, Justin Morrill somehow found the time and energy to write his greatest legislation: the Land-Grant College Act.[63]

Notes

1. Morrill to Ruth Morrill, 7 December 1860, LOC.
2. Taussig, *Tariff History*, 155.
3. McPherson, *Battle Cry of Freedom*, 213–16.
4. David M. Potter, *The Impending Crisis* (New York: Harper and Row, 1976), 442–444.
5. Ibid.; Hoyer, "Gentleman from Vermont," 121; David M. Potter, *Lincoln and His Party in the Secession Crisis* (New Haven: Yale University Press, 1962), 90.
6. Morrill to Stephen Thomas, 23 December 1860; Morrill to Ruth, 26 and 29 December 1860, and 11 January 1861, LOC.
7. Potter, *Lincoln and His Party*, 96–98.
8. Ibid., 98.
9. Ibid., 99–101.
10. Morrill to Ruth Morrill, 18 and 23 January 1861, LOC.
11. Potter, *Lincoln and His Party*, 292–93.
12. Morrill to Ruth, 1 March 1861, LOC.
13. Potter, *Lincoln and His Party*, 294–98.
14. Ibid., 298–99.
15. Morrill to Ruth Morrill, 13 February 1861; Morrill to Louise, 5 March 1861, LOC.
16. David Herbert Donald, *Lincoln* (New York, Simon and Schuster, 1995), 303–05; Morrill to Ruth, 16 April 1861, LOC.
17. Sherman, *Recollections*, 251; Dewey, *Financial History*, 276.
18. Parker, *Morrill*, 125.
19. Dewey, *Financial History*, 276–77; Sherman, *Recollections*, 257.
20. The House used the Morrill Tariff as the model for all tariff bills throughout the war.
21. Hoyer, ""Gentleman from Vermont,"" 148–50; Bray Hammond, *Sovereignty and an Empty Purse: Banks and Politics in the Civil War* (Princeton: Princeton University Press, 1970), 52.
22. Hoyer, ""Gentleman from Vermont,"" 150–51; Hammond, *Sovereignty and an Empty Purse,* 52.
23. Hoyer, "Gentleman from Vermont," 151–53; Dewey, *Financial History,* 277.
24. Hoyer, "Gentleman from Vermont," 153–54; Hammond, *Sovereignty and an Empty Purse,* 52–56; Nevins, *War for the Union,* 1: 195–96.
25. Hammond, *Sovereignty and an Empty Purse,* 52–56; J. W. Schuckers, *The Life and Public Services of Salmon Portland Chase* (New York: D. Appleton and Company, 1874), 222–23.
26. Nevins, *War for the Union,* 1: 196; Bolles, *Financial History of the United States,* 18.
27. Morrill to Ruth Morrill, 29 July 1861, LOC.
28. Schuckers, *Chase,* 230–31; Hammond, *Sovereignty and an Empty Purse,* 60–61; Bolles, *Financial History,* 36–37.
29. In November 1861 Captain Charles Wilkes of the U.S. Navy stopped the British ship *Trent* and removed two Confederate emissaries to Europe. Great Britain considered this action as an affront to their flag. Eventually, the Lincoln administration disavowed any previous knowledge of Captain Wilkes' actions and freed the prisoners.
30. Schuckers, *Chase,* 231–33; Hammond, *Sovereignty and an Empty Purse,* 133–34.
31. Schuckers, *Chase,* 233–35.

32. Nevins, *War for the Union*, vol. ii, 211; Dewey, *Financial History,* 281–82; Hammond, *Sovereignty and an Empty Purse,* 133–36.

33. Hammond, *Sovereignty and an Empty Purse,* 160–61; Schuckers, *Chase,* 235.

34. Morrill, speech, "The Impolicy of making Paper Money a Legal Tender," delivered in the House of Representatives, 4 February 1862, LOC.

35. Ibid.

36. Hammond, *Sovereignty and an Empty Purse,* 186–224; Nevins, *War for the Union,* 2: 212–13.

37. Hammond, *Sovereignty and an Empty Purse,* 269–70; Hoyer, "Gentleman from Vermont," 180.

38. Hammond, *Sovereignty and an Empty Purse,* 270–71; Hoyer, "Gentleman from Vermont," 181–82.

39. Blaine, *Twenty Years in Congress,* 1: 433.

40. Hammond, *Sovereignty and an Empty Purse,* 274–80; Hoyer, "Gentleman from Vermont," 182–82. Congress repealed the income tax in 1872, then authorized it again in 1894. The Supreme Court declared it unconstitutional in 1895. The sixteenth Amendment, adopted in 1913, made the income tax constitutional and a permanent part of the tax code.

41. Bolles, *Financial History of the United States,* 185–86; Frederic C. Howe, *Taxation and Taxes in the United States under the Internal Revenue System,* 1791–1895 (Boston: Thomas Y. Crowell and Company, 1896), 57–58.

42. Bolles, *Financial History of the United States,* 186–87; Nevins, *War for the Union,* 1: 491.

43. Wesley Clair Mitchell, *A History of the Greenbacks* (Chicago: University of Chicago Press, 1903), 82.

44. Ibid., 97–98; Hoyer, "Gentleman from Vermont," 185.

45. Parker, *Morrill,* 130–31.

46. Hoyer, "Gentleman from Vermont," 162.

47. Hammond, *Sovereignty and an Empty Purse,* 306–7; Mitchell, *History of the Greenbacks,* 106–7.

48. Mitchell, *History of the Greenbacks,* 111; Parker, *Morrill,* 144.

49. Dewey, *Financial History,* 310; Hoyer, "Gentleman from Vermont," 186–90; Hammond, *Sovereignty and an Empty Purse,* 296–305; Parker, *Morrill,* 134.

50. Morrill to Colfax, 5 May 1863, quoted in Parker, *Morrill,* 155.

51. Parker, *Morrill,* 153–58.

52. Dewey, *Financial History,* 312–13.

53. Morrill, speech, "Tax Bill," delivered in the House of Representatives, 19 April 1864, LOC.

54. Ibid.

55. Hoyer, "Gentleman from Vermont," 164–68; Stanwood, *American Tariff Controversies,* 128–29.

56. Hoyer, "Gentleman from Vermont," 135; Frederick E. Haynes, *The Reciprocity Treaty with Canada of 1854* (Baltimore: American Economic Association, 1892), 7–19.

57. Hoyer, "Gentleman from Vermont," 136, Haynes, *Reciprocity Treaty,* 20.

58. Morrill, speech, "In Favor of Terminating the Reciprocity Treaty with Great Britain," delivered in House of Representatives, 27 January 1864; Morrill, "Report on the Reciprocity Treaty," 1 March 1865, LOC.

59. Haynes, *Reciprocity Treaty,* 25–26; Morrill to H. Fish, 4 June 1874; Morrill to Sheldon, 29 November 1884; Morrill to W. Tucker, 12 May 1887; Morrill to N. Dingley, 25 September 1898, LOC.

60. Parker, *Morrill,* 151.

61. Howe, *Taxation and Taxes,* 67–68; Hoyer, "Gentleman from Vermont," 168–69.

62. Fiscal years.

63. Howe, *Taxation and Taxes,* 69.

5

Morrill's Monument: The Land-Grant College Act[1]

I am a firm believer in universal education. If the training and education of domestic animals wonderfully increases their value and title to esteem, obviously for man, having "dominion over every living creature," it must be of vastly higher importance.[2]

Justin S. Morrill

Cornell University President Andrew D. White ranked Justin Morrill's contribution to education, especially the Land-Grant College Act, with Alexander Hamilton's support of the Constitution and Thomas Jefferson's acquisition of the Louisiana Territory.[3] On the 100th anniversary of the law's enactment, Harvard Professor W. K. Jordan said, "It was responsible for the democratization of education and for the establishment of a healthy diversity in our whole structure of higher education."[4] For the same occasion, American poet Robert Frost wrote, "For me there is no greater name in American education than that of Senator Justin Smith Morrill."[5]

The memory of his own lack of opportunity undoubtedly inspired Morrill's lifelong interest in learning and education. Although largely self-taught, he was a well-educated man, especially on economics and finance, agriculture, architecture and literature. His friends included college presidents and writers. He wrote a small book entitled *Self-Consciousness of Noted Persons* with his insights on many well-known authors and philosophers. Morrill also contributed several articles to *Forum* and other magazines. With such a love for learning, it seems natural that this blacksmith's son and experimental farmer would want better educational opportunities for the children of other artisans and farmers.

Morrill was not alone in his thoughts of a more practical education for working-class families. Historian Allan Nevins said faith in progress, fueled by the social, scientific, technological, and cultural advances of the early nineteenth century, caused Americans to see the traditional college curricula as "hopelessly antiquated." The United States, and indeed the Western world, rejected classical and theological studies, championed science, insisted on classes in agriculture and mechanic arts, and demanded a "greater democracy in education."[6]

The idea for workingmen's colleges did not originate with Justin Morrill. Such institutions existed in Europe, especially in England and France, long before he ever reached Congress. Nevins credits Simeon De Witt, surveyor-general of New York, with first bringing the idea of agricultural colleges to the American public's attention. In 1819 De Witt published a pamphlet, "Considerations on the Necessity of Establishing an Agricultural College, and Having More of the Children of Wealthy Citizens Educated for the Profession of Farming," proposing a state college that included experimental research. New York Lieutenant Governor James Tallmadge recommended a School of Agricultural Mechanics and Useful Arts in 1826. In 1848 John S. Skinner petitioned Congress for subsidies for colleges of agriculture and mechanic arts.[7]

Illinois College Professor Jonathan Baldwin Turner proposed, in 1850, a new type of university. Turner's "University for the Industrial Classes" would provide a liberal education to farmers, manufacturers and workers, who composed the 99 percent ignored by traditional colleges and universities. He believed farmers could exert enough pressure on Congress to "secure for each State in the Union, an appropriation of public land adequate to create and endow in the most liberal manner, a general system of popular Industrial education, more glorious in its design and more beneficent in its results than the world has ever seen before."[8] In 1853 the Illinois legislature sent Congress a set of resolutions encapsulating Turner's ideas and asking that each state receive $500,000 worth of public land to "endow a system of industrial universities."[9]

Also, by the time Justin Morrill went to Congress, there were several American colleges that offered alternatives to the classics. The Agricultural College of Michigan and the Peoples College of New York were just two. Closer to home, West Point's former commandant Captain Alden Partridge had begun an academy, which grew into Norwich

University, at Norwich, Vermont, just twelve miles from Strafford. In 1841 Partridge petitioned Congress to establish a national education system that taught not only liberal arts, but farming, engineering and commerce. Morrill had to be familiar with Partridge's ideas because Judge Harris was a Norwich Academy incorporator and a trustee until his death. The school asked Morrill to be a trustee in 1848, but he declined citing the institution's lax standards for awarding honorary degrees.[10]

Morrill himself recounted how he came to write his famous bill. Shortly after taking office in December 1855, he noticed the older states received little benefit from large public land grants. Also, productivity of eastern and northern land was rapidly decreasing, while English soil, under more scientific cultivation, maintained its productivity. He reasoned, therefore, that the United States could benefit from institutions similar to those in England that taught agricultural and mechanical arts. American colleges offered instruction almost exclusively for doctors, lawyers and ministers. Morrill concluded that a curriculum focused on practical sciences "would do the greatest good to the greatest number."[11]

Congressman Morrill gave the first hint of his interest in a practical education for the working-class, on 28 February 1856. He offered a resolution asking the Committee on Agriculture to establish a "Board of Agriculture" and "one or more national agricultural schools upon the basis of the naval and military academies." One student from each Congressional district and two from each state at large could "receive a scientific and practical education at the public expense" at the new schools.[12] Congressman Lawrence Keitt of South Carolina, however, objected and the committee refused to receive the resolution.[13]

This failure apparently only stimulated Morrill's thoughts of agricultural colleges. He discussed the idea of using federal land grants to finance such institutions with William Hebard, a former Second District congressman. Hebard endorsed the proposal, but did not believe Congress would approve it. When Morrill approached members of Congress with his idea, they echoed Hebard's response, "You can try, but of course it is of no use." Such reaction would have "killed the project," he recalled, except many also added they would vote for such a bill.[14]

Morrill introduced the Bill Granting Lands for Agricultural Colleges on 17 December 1857. He made a motion to refer it to the Committee on Agriculture, of which he was a member. Virginian John Letcher proposed the Committee on Public Lands instead. Letcher's motion carried 105 to 89. Morrill knew that committee's chair Williamson R. W. Cobb and most of its members opposed the measure. He hoped, however, a strong minority report would allow the bill to proceed to the House floor. While the bill was in committee, Morrill and his friends in the House polled other members and learned it had enough support to pass a vote in the entire House. Reverend Amos Brown, President of New York's Peoples College and "Col. Wilder," President of the National Agricultural Society, came to Washington and "zealously" encouraged House members to vote for the bill.[15]

Indeed, when Chairman Cobb reported the bill out of committee on 15 April 1858, the majority had recommended rejecting it. Showing an adroitness lacking just a year before when he introduced anti-polygamy legislation, Morrill and two allies, David Walbridge of Michigan and Israel Washburn of Maine whom Morrill considered the best parliamentarian in the House, maneuvered to keep the measure before the House. Morrill received permission to speak on the bill in the next morning session. Walbridge, who had presented a favorable minority report from committee, moved to postpone consideration. Washburn then made a motion to return the bill to the Committee on Public Lands. These actions ensured opponents could not quickly kill the bill. At the next morning session on April 20 when Morrill rose to claim the floor, Walbridge and Washburn withdrew their motions. Morrill then offered an amendment, almost identical to the original bill, as a substitute for his measure. The amendment became the pending floor business. This allowed him to deliver his speech supporting the bill.[16]

Morrill first considered the constitutionality of his measure. The federal government, he noted, spent millions on lighthouses, coast surveys, harbor improvements, and support for the Navy and Naval Academy, all for the benefit of commerce. Railroads had received immense land grants to expand internal trade. Authors and inventors benefited from copyrights and patents. Large land grants had also boosted general education. "But all direct encouragement to agriculture has been rigidly withheld."[17]

He next addressed American agriculture's declining productivity. Statistics showed New England wheat production had dropped from 2,014,111 bushels in 1840 to 1,090,132 in 1850. During the same period, potato production shrank from 35,180,500 to 19,418,191 bushels. Figures from southern states showed similar trends. Virginia grew eighteen million fewer pounds of tobacco in 1850 than in 1840. Decreasing yields showed a "wide-spread deterioration of the soil" with proportionate loss of capital and wages. "Our country is growing debilitated, and we propagate the consumptive disease with all the energy of private enterprise and public patronage." Morrill asked, "Does not our general system of agriculture foreshadow ultimate decay? If so, is it beyond our constitutional power and duty to provide an incidental remedy?"[18]

The cause of this downward spiral, Morrill believed, was lack of knowledge and skill. Only the federal government could reverse this trend. Foreign governments aided agriculture and the results were impressive. Belgium, for example, supported a population of 336 per square mile compared to Virginia's 23 people per square mile. [Belgium's] "once noted battle-fields are now equally noted model farms." France spared no expense on agricultural science. French botanical gardens, veterinary schools, five agricultural colleges and nearly one hundred "inferior agricultural schools" "surpass[ed] all others in existence." England had several agricultural schools and colleges, but "jealousies of caste" kept the enrollment low. Although the United States had ninety-five times the land of England and seventeen times that of Belgium, America had imported over $100 million in agricultural products the previous year.[19]

He continued, "We have schools to teach the art of manslaying and make masters of 'deep-throated engines' of war; and shall we not have schools to teach men the way to feed, clothe, and enlighten the great brotherhood of man?" Agricultural colleges would not compete with literary colleges since each would serve separate needs. Farmers and "mechanics"[20] needed specialized schools and literature "quite as much as the so-called learned professions." In agricultural colleges, farmers could learn the capability of soils and the benefits of various fertilizers, which grasses produced the best livestock and the most milk, deep plowing and drainage methods, remedies for crop diseases, and how to control insects. Tuition would be free, while the sale of crops could help defray expenses.[21]

The sale of public lands, lands that "should be considered *a common fund for the use and benefit of all*," would finance the colleges. Each state would receive 20,000 acres of public land for each representative and senator. The government had previously awarded 45,109,879 acres to veterans. New states had received generous grants. Ten states and one territory had received 25,403,993 acres since 1850 to build railroads. By 1857, 67,736,572 acres had gone to states and territories for schools and universities. Morrill estimated under his bill approximately 5.8 million acres would go to agricultural colleges, leaving more than one billion acres of public land. In recommending the measure's passage, he urged, "Let it never be said we are 'the greatest and the meanest of mankind'."[22]

After Morrill had delivered a speech that he considered "was probably something better than [his] friends expected," Cobb presented his committee's adverse report and spoke against the bill. Morrill then obtained the floor and members friendly to the bill "demanded the previous question upon its passage." Cobb made a motion to return the bill to committee, but that failed by a vote of 83 to 114. Another motion to table the measure lost 83 to 105. Finally, after some filibustering and other delays, the House passed the bill 105 votes to 100.[23]

It then moved to the upper house where Michigan Senator Charles E. Stuart attempted to guide it through. He tried to bring the bill to a vote without debate, but opponents delayed the vote until the next session. Stuart faltered in attempts to bring the bill up for a vote when Congress reconvened in December 1858. On 1 February 1859, Benjamin Wade of Ohio replaced Stuart as the bill's sponsor in the Senate. Southerners, clinging to the safety of a narrow interpretation of the Constitution, bitterly opposed the measure. Clement Clay, of Alabama, called it "one of the most monstrous, iniquitous and dangerous measures which have ever been submitted to Congress."[24] James Mason, of Virginia, labeled the bill "one of the most extraordinary engines of mischief," a misuse of federal property, and "an unconstitutional robbing of the Treasury for the purpose of bribing the States."[25] Wade's Ohio colleague George Pugh said the bill involved "as atrocious a violation of the organic law as if it were the act of an armed usurper."[26] Although Jefferson Davis of Mississippi, Henry Rice of Minnesota, and other southerners and westerners opposed the bill, Wade pushed it to a vote. On February 7 the Senate passed the measure with two minor amendments 25 to 22. The House then approved the amended version 148 to 95 on February 16 and sent it to President James Buchanan.[27]

Morrill's bill received wide support among voters, not only in Vermont, but throughout the country. Pliny H. White, an Amherst, Massachusetts, newspaper editor, worked to "create a healthy publich sentiment" for the bill. An Illinois farmer admitted his ignorance of the soil he cultivated and hoped Morrill's efforts would be "crowned with success." Iowa Republicans applauded Morrill's efforts and requested copies of his speech. Farmers in Kansas and Michigan also wrote expressing their gratitude. An Ohio writer suggested Morrill review Buchanan's voting record in the Senate on previous land-grant measures to help secure the president's endorsement of this one.[28]

Morrill had already studied Buchanan's voting record and discovered he had voted for a land-grant for a school for the hearing-impaired. So it seemed likely the president would endorse the Land-Grant College Bill. When Buchanan had not signed the bill after a week, Morrill grew apprehensive. On February 24 New York Representative Daniel Sickles, who had been Buchanan's secretary in London, asked Morrill for a copy of his speech. Sickles wanted to remind the president of his previous position and to persuade him to sign the bill. Sickles hurried to the White House with the speech, but soon return disappointed. He told Morrill he had been too late. Democratic senators, led by John Slidell of Louisiana, had already convinced Buchanan to veto the bill. The president justified his veto by arguing the measure was both inexpedient and unconstitutional. Morrill refuted Buchanan's claims, but accepted the fact that without enough votes to override the veto the Land-Grant College Act was dead until after the 1860 presidential election.[29]

Morrill knew his "College Land Bill" had widespread support among the American people. Thirteen states had instructed their representatives and senators to vote for the measure when it came up again. When Abraham Lincoln was elected president in 1860 prospects looked good. Pressing Civil War matters, however, took precedent. On 16 December 1861, Morrill reintroduced a revised version of his earlier bill. "Without excluding other scientific and classical studies," the colleges' curricula would include agriculture, mechanical arts [engineering], and military tactics. Morrill increased the land allotment from 20 to 30 thousand acres for each representative and senator and, probably inspired by recent Union defeats, included a provision for teaching military tactics. The new bill also excluded territories and rebelling states.[30]

The House referred the bill to the Committee on Public Lands. After a delay of nearly six months, committee chair John Fox Potter of Wisconsin reported the measure on 29 May 1862, with a "do not pass" recommendation. Westerners opposed having public lands in their states sold to build eastern schools. They also believed speculators would buy large tracts and let them sit idle while waiting for prices to rise.[31]

During the long delay, while the House Committee on Public Lands considered the measure, Morrill gave a copy to his friend "Old Ben" Wade and asked him to introduce it in the Senate. Wade presented the bill on May 2 and shepherded it through the upper house. Again, westerners, led by Kansas Senator James Lane, resisted. Fearing that outsiders would claim all Kansas' prime public lands before the state could reserve lands for schools, Lane sought to restrict the agricultural college land-grants to the territories. Lane considered the bill the "most iniquitous" to the western states of any measure ever introduced into Congress. "In it is contained the ruin of the State that I . . . represent."[32] Henry Rice, of Minnesota, predicted that speculators would grab the best land, "blighting, like the locusts, every region which may attract them."[33] Wade countered that the federal government had treated western states generously and denied any state's special claim to federal lands within its boundaries. Iowa Senator James Harlan also refuted Lane's argument. Harlan pointed out even if *all* the land claimed came from Kansas, the state would still have immense acreage remaining. Lane then offered an amendment limiting the land claimed in any one state to one million acres. Wade accepted the proposal and the bill passed the Senate on June 10 by a 32–7 vote.[34]

After the House Committee on Public Lands had reported negatively on Morrill's bill, he unsuccessfully tried to introduce a substitute measure. When the Senate version came to the House on 17 June Morrill told his colleagues everyone already understood the measure since it had been before Congress and the country for the preceding five years. After several attempts to amend or delay the bill failed, the House approved the "College Land Bill" 90 to 25. President Lincoln signed it into law on 2 July 1862.[35]

Under the act, each state received 30,000 acres of public land for each of its representatives and senators in Congress. In western states, where public land still existed, public officials would select actual parcels of land. The state could either sell it immediately or hold it until prices increased. States with no public lands received scrip, which they had to sell to assignees to prevent one state from owning land in another. Assignees then could redeem the scrip for actual parcels of land. The states would create a "perpetual fund" by investing the proceeds from the land or scrip sales in "stocks of the United States or of the States, or some other safe stocks, yielding not less than five per centum." The fund's capital would "remain forever undiminished." Income from the investments would pay "the endowment, support, and maintenance of at least one college" in each state. In describing the federal and state roles in building land-grant institutions, Morrill said, "The bounty of the national government formed a nucleus in the several states around which buildings, libraries, laboratories, museums, workshops, gymnasiums, military halls and other educational appliances were expected to be assembled, from funds derived from other and independent sources."

States had to agree to the law's provisions within two years and establish a college within five years.[36]

Although several states, led by Iowa, quickly accepted the conditions of the Land-Grant College Act and moved to create colleges, initial progress was slow. One reason was the flood of federal land that came onto the market simultaneously. Eventually, the colleges received 17,430,000 acres under the act. The Homestead Act, which Lincoln also signed on 2 July 1862, gave settlers 160 acres of public land. Only one day earlier, he had approved a transcontinental railroad bill giving large tracts to the Union Pacific and Central Pacific Railroads. Eventually, claimants acquired 70 million acres of prairie farmland under the Homestead Act and another 130 million acres passed to builders of the transcontinental railroad. Veterans of the Mexican War and various skirmishes against the Indians had already received warrants for over 61 million acres.[37]

Many states sold their scrip during this glutted market and received less than one dollar an acre. Cornell University, New York's land-grant institution, held its grant until the market improved and received $5,765,000, or $5.82 an acre. But only nine states received more than $1.25 an acre. Total proceeds only reached $7.5 million. Furthermore, states often had little money for buildings since the bill passed during the Civil War. Also, because the new colleges had few teachers and limited curricula, very few students applied for courses in agriculture or mechanical arts.[38]

One positive result from the act was the creation of colleges for African-Americans. Mississippi's Alcorn State University became the first black land-grant university in 1871. Virginia's Hampton University became a land-grant institution in 1872. Booker T. Washington, founder of Tuskegee Institute, graduated from Hampton.[39] Frederick Douglas wrote Morrill, "I see no great or happy future for my race or for the Republic outside general education and its seems to me that you, dear sir, standing where you do can do no better work for the nation than to press this idea upon the nation's mind and heart." Unfortunately, most southern states with the largest African-American populations initially declined to share land-grant funds with the recently freed slaves.[40]

Although progress was slow for all the land-grant colleges, Morrill remained steadfast in his faith and support. He helped incorporate the University of Vermont in 1865 and served many years as a trustee. In his role as trustee, Morrill solicited aid from the state legislature. Also, in 1872 he proposed creating a permanent educational fund from the sale of public lands to help maintain the land-grant colleges. When this measure failed to pass, he tried again, and again, and again. Between 1872 and 1890 Morrill brought forward seven bills to aid the land-grant colleges. In 1890 he argued an additional land-grant would not interfere with free homesteads, preemption, experiment stations or future legislation governing railroads. The 1862 law had created 48 colleges that were "sending forth a large number of vigorous young men to scientific, agricultural, mechanical, educational, and other industrial careers." The previous law had "borne healthy and excellent fruit," but the colleges needed more money. This time Morrill carried the day. President Benjamin Harrison signed the second Land Grant Act into law on 30 August 1890.[41]

This second act gave states an additional $15,000 a year initially for their land-grant colleges. This amount gradually increased to $25,000 a year. Although the land-grant colleges in most states were open to African-American students and many took advantage of the opportunity, discrimination and segregation prompted most black families to send their children to segregated southern black colleges, especially for their undergraduate degree. The second Land-Grant College act also mandated that colleges "where a distinction of race or color is made in the admission of students" would receive no money. But, simultaneously, it allowed "equal-but-separate" institutions. Colored Normal, Industrial, Agricultural and Mechanical College of South Carolina (later renamed South Carolina State University) and State Normal School for Colored Persons (later renamed Kentucky State University) became land-grant colleges in 1896 and 1897. By 1997 seventeen predominantly African-American land-grant colleges and universities had awarded over 700 thousand degrees.[42]

Even with the additional funding from the 1890 bill, Morrill was not content. In 1897 he failed in another attempt to win more money for the colleges. As late as November 1898, he was planning the best time to approach Congress for another increase. He believed he should wait until "the people have learned and appreciated the large number of soldiers and officers that were furnished by the Land Grant Colleges" in the Spanish-American War.[43]

After Morrill's death Edmund J. James, University of Illinois President, questioned Morrill's authorship and responsibility for the Land-Grant College Act of 1862. James claimed Jonathan B. Turner, who had coincidentally taught at Illinois College, was the "real father of the so-called Morrill Act." James based his assertion on Turner's history of support for "industrial colleges," similarities in some wording between the act and some of Turner's writings, and a short letter from Morrill to Turner. Such evidence proved, according to James, Turner and other supporters "selected" Morrill to introduce the bill "because he was from an older state which had not thus far benefited by the land grant of the Federal Government."[44]

Certainly the idea for federally-sponsored education or colleges specializing in agriculture and mechanical arts did not originate with Justin Morrill. King James granted ten thousand acres to Virginia in 1618 for a college. A federal law in 1785 reserved one section in each township to maintain public schools. As previously stated, the Agricultural College of Michigan and the People's College of New York were offering courses directed toward the working class before Morrill introduced his legislation. Also, several European nations had government-sponsored, agriculturally-oriented institutions long before 1858. Indeed, Turner was a strong advocate for federally-sponsored "industrial" colleges. But so was Alden Partridge of Norwich University, near Morrill's home in Vermont. James made sweeping assertions based on little evidence. The similar wording was confined to *one sentence*. The letter from Morrill to Turner that "proved" their close friendship contained six lines, in which Morrill "presumed" he recognized Professor Turner, "an old pioneer in the cause of agricultural education." He also told Turner, "I have faith that I shall get *my* [emphasis added] bill into law at this session."[45] Morrill must have been familiar with Turner's ideas for he had attended the 1856 Agricultural Society meeting that included a full discussion of Turner's plan. There is, however, no evidence in Morrill's papers that Turner had any direct influence in the writing or passage of the Land-Grant College Act. Historian Earle Ross, in arguing against Turner's influence, cites an 1872 letter from Turner to Morrill stating, "You may not know or you may have forgotten . . . that I have always felt a deep interest in this subject and watch its progress with great solicitude."[46] In fact, Morrill, himself, said, "I do not remember of any assistance in framing my bill prior to its introduction."[47] Ross considered Morrill's bill a synthesis of numerous past proposals, "the epitome of two decades of regional agitation and experimentation."[48]

Although some people might doubt Morrill's authorship of the Land-Grant College Act, there can be no question about the bill's contribution to this country. Officers trained under the military training provision of the 1862 act fought in the Spanish-American War and World War I. When World War II began over 50,000 Army Reserve Officer Training

Corps (ROTC) officers, trained at land-grant colleges, helped America mobilize. Army Chief of Staff General George C. Marshall said, "Just what we would have done in the early phases of our training and mobilization without these men I do not know."[49] In 1954 President Dwight D. Eisenhower applauded the land-grant colleges' military training: "I am one of those who can bear sincere witness to the efficacy of that training and to the very great services you people and your predecessors have rendered to the United States of America on the field of battle."[50]

The act has contributed greatly to America's higher education. In 1994 29 tribal colleges joined the land-grant system increasing the total to 104 (see chart 1 for the complete list). Three million students attended land-grant colleges and universities in 1997, including about 150 thousand at the nine campuses of the University of California, the largest, and fewer than 2.5 thousand at Kentucky State University, the smallest university. The land-grant institutions have granted 20 million degrees, including one-third of all masters degrees and more than half of all doctorates. The land-grant schools also produced eleven American presidents.[51]

But the land-grant institutions' contributions go beyond mere statistics. By emphasizing agriculture, mechanics (engineering) and other practical courses, these schools broadened the scope of American education. Morrill wrote that "without excluding other scientific and classical studies" land-grant colleges should teach "military tactics" and "branches of learning . . . related to agriculture and the mechanic arts . . . in order to promote the liberal and practical education of the industrial classes."[52] This left room for wide interpretation. "Agriculture" came to include forestry, home economics and veterinary medicine. "Mechanic arts" included all branches of engineering. Ezra Cornell, founder of Cornell University, believed the land-grant school should allow any student to study any subject.[53] Historian Edward Eddy said, "With its vocational emphasis, [the Land-Grant College Act] forced education to conform to the growing American outlook of utilitarianism."[54]

Before 1862 America's university students were affluent, white males. Land-grant colleges opened the door of higher education to women, blacks, the working classes, immigrants and other minorities. Eddy explained, the 1862 law "forced education to fit the changing social and economic patterns of an expanding nation. It helped to create equality of educational opportunity by offering education at public expense to the industrial classes; it gave some measure of dignity to the vocations pursued by such classes."[55]

Most land-grant schools were coeducational and multiracial from the beginning, except in the South. Morrill's second Land-Grant College Act in 1890 provided money for "separate-but-equal" black colleges throughout the South. Since southern states would not spend the money for two separate black colleges, the black land-grant colleges were all coeducational from the beginning.[56] Iowa State University President A. S. Welch supported coeducation saying, "Sexual isolation for the purpose of culture is contrary to nature; it makes boys rough and girls silly."[57]

Through an "open door" policy, land-grant colleges allowed students with deficient or substandard high school records to enter on probationary status. A University of Kansas survey showed that such students accounted for 20 percent of the graduating class, including one Phi Beta Kappa and several on the dean's honor roll. The nonsectarian land-grant colleges also separated religion from higher education and helped establish research as a function of American universities.[58] Justin Morrill displayed great vision in writing the land-grant college acts and fighting for their support. That vision continued to expand and gained more clarity as Morrill and the colleges matured. In 1893 he said,

> Asking personally for nothing, . . . I trust it may be believed that I have aimed only to promote 'the greatest good for the greatest number,' and to construe the college act of 1862 in its true sense and meaning, by which only can its greatest usefulness and highest service to our State and to the whole country be fully developed and preserved.[59]

At a celebration of the 50th anniversary of the Land-Grant College Act, William Oxley Thompson, president of Ohio State University, summed up his vision of his land-grant institution's purpose and contribution. The university should focus on "the good it can do," on "the people it can serve," on "the science it can promote," and on "the civilization it can advance." After quoting another college president whose purpose was "to take only 'prepared men' and 'teach them the essentials,'" Thompson said the land-grant universities took "unprepared men and made leaders of them."[60]

Although the enactment of the 1862 Land-Grant College Act must have pleased Morrill, he had little time to bask in his success. He was too busy helping the Union finance the Civil War. Then immediately after the war ended, he began the long, tedious process of restoring the tax and tariff system to a peace time footing. He started the process in the House of Representatives, but after 1867 he continued his efforts in the Senate.

Alabama: Alabama A & M University, Auburn University, Tuskegee University.

Alaska: University of Alaska Statewide System.

American Samoa: Community College of American Samoa.

Arizona: University of Arizona, Navajo Community College.

Arkansas: University of Arkansas, Fayetteville, University of Arkansas, Pine Bluff.

California: University of California System, D-Q University.

Colorado: Colorado State University.

Connecticut: University of Connecticut.

Delaware: Delaware State University, University of Delaware.

District of Columbia: University of the District of Columbia.

Florida: Florida A & M University, University of Florida.

Georgia: Fort Valley State College, University of Georgia.

Guam: University of Guam.

Hawaii: University of Hawaii.

Idaho: University of Idaho.

Illinois: University of Illinois.

Indiana: Purdue University.

Iowa: Iowa State University.

Kansas: Kansas State University, Haskell Indian Nations University.

Kentucky: Kentucky State University, University of Kentucky.

Louisiana: Louisiana State University System, Southern University System.

Maine: University of Maine.

Maryland: University of Maryland at College Park, University of Maryland Eastern Shore.

Massachusetts: Massachusetts Institute of Technology, University of Massachusetts.

Michigan: Bay Mills Community College, Michigan Stacte University.

Micronesia: Community College of Micronesia—FSM.

Minnesota: University of Minnesota, Fond du Lac Community College, Leech Lake Tribal College.

Mississippi: Alcorn State University, Mississippi State University.

Missouri: Lincoln University, University of Missouri System.

Montana: Montana State University, Blackfeet Community College, Dull Knife Community College, Fort Belknap Community College, Fort Peck Community College, Little Bighorn College, Salish Kootenai College, Stone Child College.

Nebraska: University of Nebraska System, Nebraska Indian Community College.

Nevada: University of Nevada, Reno.

New Hampshire: University of New Hampshire.

New Jersey: Rutgers, the State University of New Jersey.

New Mexico: New Mexico State University, Crownpoint Institute of Technology, Institute of American Indian and Alaska Native Culture Arts Development, Southwest Indian Polytechnic Institute.

New York: Cornell University.

North Carolina: North Carolina A & T State University, North Carolina State University.

North Dakota: North Dakota State University, Fort Bethold Community College, Little Hoop Community College, Standing Rock College, Turtle Mountain Community College, United Tribes Technical College.

Northern Marianas: Northern Marianas College.

Ohio: Ohio State University.

Oklahoma: Langston University, Oklahoma State University.

Oregon: Oregon State University.

Pennsylvania: Pennsylvania State University.

Puerto Rico: University of Puerto Rico.

Rhode Island: University of Rhode Island.

South Carolina: Clemson University, South Carolina State University.

South Dakota: South Dakota State University, Cheyenne River Community College, Ogalala Lakota College, Sinte Gleska University, Sisseton Wahpeton Community College.

Tennessee: Tennessee State University, University of
Tennessee.

Texas: Prairie View A & M University, Texas A & M
University.

Utah: Utah State University.

Vermont: University of Vermont.

Virgin Islands: University of Virgin Islands.

Virginia: Virginia Polytechnic Institute and State
University, Virginia State University, American
Indian Higher Education Consortium.

Washington: Washington State University, Northwest Indian
College.

West Virginia: West Virginia University.

Wisconsin: University of Wisconsin-Madison, College of
the Menominee Nation, Lac Courte Ojibwa
Community College.

Wyoming: University of Wyoming.[61]

Notes

1. The official title: An Act donating Public Lands to the several States and Territories which may provide Colleges for the benefit of Agriculture and the Mechanic Arts.
2. Morrill, speech, delivered at University of Vermont, 28 June 1893, LOC.
3. Parker, *Morrill*, 259.
4. *After 100 Years: A Report by the State of Vermont Morrill Land-Grant Centennial Committee, 1962*, 13.
5. Ibid., 14.
6. Allan Nevins, *The Origins of the Land-Grant Colleges and State Universities* (Washington DC: Civil War Centennial Commission, 1962), 7.
7. Ibid., 18.
8. Ibid.; Russell I. Thackrey and Jay Richter, "The Land-Grant Colleges and Universities, 1862–1962, An American Institution," *Higher Education*, 16, no.3 (Nov. 1959): 5.
9. Ibid.
10. Hoyer, "Gentleman from Vermont," 49–50; Morrill to J. Davis, 8 December 1848, LOC.
11. Morrill to W. T. Hewett, 5 February 1894, LOC.
12. Parker, *Morrill*, 82.
13. Hoyer, "Gentleman from Vermont," 34.
14. Parker, *Morrill*, 262–63; Morrill to W. T. Hemett, 5 February 1894.
15. Parker, *Morrill*, 264; Morrill to Hemett, 5 February 1894.
16. Parker, *Morrill*, 265; Hoyer, "Gentleman from Vermont," 56–57; Morrill to Hemett, 5 February 1894.

17. Morrill, speech, "Bill Granting Lands for Agricultural Colleges," delivered in the House of Representatives, 20 April 1858, LOC.

18. Ibid.

19. Ibid.

20. The term used for all craftsmen.

21. Morrill, speech, "Bill Granting Lands for Agricultural Colleges," delivered 20 April 1858.

22. Ibid.

23. Parker, *Morrill*, 265–66; Hoyer, "Gentleman from Vermont," 58–61; Morrill to Hemett, 5 February 1894; George Atherton, speech, "The Legislative Career of Justin S. Morrill," 14 November 1900, LOC.

24. Paul W. Gates, "Western Opposition to the Agricultural College Act," *Indiana Magazine of History*, 37 (March 1941): 107.

25. Ibid.

26. Ibid.

27. Parker, *Morrill*, 266–67; Hoyer, "Gentleman from Vermont," 61–63; Atherton, speech, "Legislative Career."

28. P. H. White to Morrill, 2 January 1858; C. G. Raymond to Morrill, 14 January 1858; N. L. Young to Morrill, 1 February 1858; E. Whittling to Morrill, 14 May 1858; J. Sherrington to Morrill, 17 May 1858; O. D. Hale to Morrill, 16 October 1858, LOC.

29. Parker, *Morrill*, 268–69; Hoyer, "Gentleman from Vermont," 64–66; Atherton, "Legislative Career"; Morrill to Hemett, 5 February 1894.

30. Atherton, "Legislative Career"; Parker, *Morrill*, 268–69; Hoyer, "Gentleman from Vermont," 68–69; Morrill to Hemett, 5 February 1894; Gates, "Western Opposition," 104–36.

31. Parker, *Morrill*, 268–69; Hoyer, "Gentleman from Vermont," 68–69; Atherton, speech, "Legislative Career"; Morrill to Hemett, 5 February 1894; Gates, "Western Opposition," 104–36.

32. Gates, "Western Opposition," 111.

33. Ibid.

34. Parker, *Morrill*, 270; Hoyer, "Gentleman from Vermont," 69–70; Atherton, speech, "Legislative Career"; Morrill to Hewett, 5 February 1894.

35. Parker, *Morrill*, 270–71; Hoyer, "Gentleman from Vermont," 72–73; Atherton, speech, "Legislative Career."

36. Morrill, speech, "State Aid to Land Grant Colleges," delivered, Montpelier, Vt., 10 October 1888, LOC; Atherton, speech, "Legislative Career"; John T. Wahlquist and James W. Thornton, Jr., *State Colleges and Universities* (Washington D.C.: The Center for Applied Research in Education, Inc., 1964), 8–9; Gates, "Western Opposition," 106.

37. Parker, *Morrill*, 271–72; Allan Nevins, *The State Universities and Democracy* (Urbana: University of Illinois Press, 1962), 34–35; Gates, "Western Opposition," 110; Cross, *Go West*, 68, 111.

38. Ibid.

39. Yvonne Freeman, "The Formation of the Black Land-Grant Colleges," 1992, unpublished, copy at Morrill Homestead, Strafford, Vermont.

40. Douglas to Morrill, 4 January 1880, LOC.

41. Morrill, speech, "Colleges for the Benefit of Agriculture and the Mechanic Arts," delivered in the Senate, 14 June 1890, LOC; Thackrey and Richter, "The Land-Grant Colleges and Universities," 3–20.

42. Thackrey and Richter, "Land-Grant Colleges and Universities," 3–20; Ralph D. Christy and Lionel Williamson, eds., *A Century of Service; Land-Grant Colleges and Universities, 1890–1990* (New Brunswick: Transaction Publishers, 1992), 4, 15–16; *Land For Learning: Justin Morrill and America's Land-Grant Colleges and Universities,* video, (Vermont ETV, 1997). Although not originally a land-grant college, Tuskegee University also shares in the benefits of the 1890 act.

43. Morrill to M. H. Buckham, 30 November 1898, LOC.

44. Edmund J. James, *The Origin of the Land Grant Act of 1862* (the so-called Morrill Act) (Urbana: University of Illinois, 1910), 7–36.

45. Morrill to J. B. Turner, 30 December 1861, quoted in James, *Land Grant Act of 1862.*

46. Earle D. Ross, *Democracy's College: The Land-Grant Movement in the Formative Stage* (Ames: The Iowa State College Press, 1942), 53.

47. Parker, *Morrill,* 262–63; Morrill to W. T. Hemett, 5 February 1894.

48. Ross, *Democracy's College,* 46.

49. Herman R. Allen, *Open Door to Learning: The Land-Grant System Enters Its Second Century* (Urbana: University of Illinois Press, 1963), 171–72,

50. Quoted by Edward Danforth Eddy, Jr., *Colleges for Our Land and Time: The Land-Grant Idea in American Education* (New York: Harper and Brothers, 1956), 274.

51. "After 100 Years," 3; Office of Public Affairs, National Association of State Universities and Land-Grant Colleges, January 94, Morrill Homestead; National Association of State Universities and Land-Grant Colleges, Fall 1993 Enrollment at Public, Four-Year Institutions, October 1994, 27–29; video, *Land for Learning.*

52. Russell I. Thackrey, *The Future of the State University* (Urbana: University of Illinois Press, 1971), 8–9.

53. Ibid., 8–13.

54. Eddy, *Colleges for Our Land and Time,* 45.

55. Ibid.

56. Ibid., 16–19.

57. Thackrey, *The Future of the State University,* 14–16.

58. Ibid., 19–27.

59. Morrill, speech, "The Land Grant Colleges," delivered at Burlington, 28 June 1893, LOC.

60. Ibid.

61. Office of Public Affairs, National Association of State Universities and Land-Grant Colleges.

Justin Smith Morrill
around the time of his wedding, 1851. Courtesy of the
National Archives.

Mrs. Justin Morrill's wedding photograph. Ruth Barrell Swan mar-
ried Justin Morrill 17 September 1851 at her family home in Easton,
Massachusetts. Courtesy of the Vermont Division for Historic
Preservation, Montpelier, Vermont.

The Morrill homestead in Strafford, Vermont. This Gothic Revival house was designed by Morrill and built between 1848–53. Currently, the site is a state-owned historic site. Courtesy of the Vermont Division for Historic Preservation, Montpelier, Vermont.

Strafford, Vermont today with the Morrill homestead in the foreground. Courtesy of the Vermont Division for Historic Preservation, Montpelier, Vermont.

The library at the Morrill homestead in Strafford, Vermont. Courtesy of the Vermont Division for Historic Preservation, Montpelier, Vermont.

The home of Senator Morrill at One Thomas Circle in Washington, D.C. was built circa 1876 under the direction of Mr. Clark, known as the "Architect of the Capital." Courtesy of the Vermont Division for Historic Preservation, Montpelier, Vermont.

A view from the drawing room, looking into the dining room, of Senator Morrill's house at One Thomas Circle. Courtesy of the Vermont Division for Historic Preservation, Montpelier, Vermont.

Justin Morrill, his wife Ruth, the dog Trump, his son James, and his sister-in-law Louise Swan on the south porch of their homestead in Strafford, Vermont, circa 1890. Courtesy of the Vermont Division for Historic Preservation, Montpelier, Vermont.

James S. Morrill with his dog Trump and horse behind the Morrill homestead in Strafford, Vermont. The weathervane in the background is on the Morrill cow barn. Courtesy of the Vermont Division for Historic Preservation, Montpelier, Vermont.

An engraving of Morrill. Courtesy of the Vermont Division for Historic Preservation, Montpelier, Vermont.

An original charcoal drawing of Ruth B. Swan Morrill at the Morrill homestead in Strafford, Vermont. Courtesy of the Vermont Division for Historic Preservation, Montpelier, Vermont.

6

THE POLITICIAN INSIDE THE PUBLIC SERVANT

I know of no one more capable of filling the vacancy in the United States Senate occasioned by the death of the lamented Jacob Collamer than Justin S. Morrill. His large experience as a legislator, his practical good sense and his inflexible honesty of purpose would seem to point to him as the man of all others . . .on the score of national interest, state interest, and self interest, who should receive the united suffrage of the freemen of Vermont.

M. W. C. Wright[1]

With the end of the Civil War, Morrill faced the task of dismantling the revenue programs that financed the victory. Before the Thirty-eighth Congress ended in March 1865, Representative Samuel Cox of Ohio initiated a rule change that divided the Ways and Means Committee into Ways and Means, Appropriations, and Banking and Currency. When the Thirty-ninth Congress convened in December 1865, Justin Morrill accepted the Ways and Means chair. But, even as he assumed the position, Morrill planned to try for the Senate.[2]

In late 1865 seventy-three year-old Senator Jacob Collamer's health began to fail. Morrill assumed the senator would not run for reelection in 1866. Morrill admired Collamer and considered him a friend and a role model. Three years earlier, Senator Collamer had said, "Mr. Morrill is the best man you can send to the Senate from Eastern Vermont."[3]

Morrill looked like a senator "should" look. He was fifty-five, tall and lean. He had a full head of graying hair that extended into "mutton-chop" sideburns. A contemporary writer for *The Independent* described him as a tall gentleman with scholarly stooped shoulders. "That stoop comes of working . . . for years over miles of tax-bills. . . . The clear eyes to be seen above these shoulders reflect the large intelligence . . . the integrity and the goodness of the man. Here is a face to believe in without reservation."[4]

Assessing his own qualifications to be senator, Morrill wrote a friend to "pardon the egotism" but, confidentially, he believed he had as much influence in the House as former speaker Nathaniel Banks or Republican Party leader James G. Blaine. Morrill considered Thaddeus Stevens "a remarkable man, unequalled in a great many respects in the history of the world." But, he added, "I have had a good many contest with him . . . and have been rarely worsted."[5]

In early November 1865, Senator Collamer died. On 10 November, Morrill confided his intention to run for Collamer's seat to his friend C. W. Willard, editor of the *Green Mountain Freeman*. Morrill explained, "I shall be a candidate. I should not be but for the fact that many friends assure me that the people of the state to a large extent will expect it and they also say it will not be a doubtful contest. All of my present colleagues including even the late Senator Collamer are openly in my favor."[6] He also solicited Willard's support, if the editor considered him as the best candidate. But, if Willard thought Judge Luke Poland would "do the state the most service—say so unflinchingly. The state is entitled to so much and I shall cheerfully acquiesce in the verdict of the state."[7]

Vermont Supreme Court Chief Justice Luke Poland, an ex-Democrat, was the other leading Republican candidate. While acknowledging that former governor J. Gregory Smith and several other influential Vermont Republicans would support Poland, Morrill felt confident the "present best men in the state" would back his own candidacy. He, therefore, surveyed his friends to learn if they supported his election to the Senate.[8]

Justin Morrill considered himself a public servant, who placed the wishes of the voters ahead of his own. Although he probably would have disavowed the label, he was also an astute and very effective politician. Even before holding public office, he worked within the Whig party strengthening the organization and garnering support for national and local candidates. He also gave speeches and wrote editorials espousing the Whig position on important issues. Ten years in Congress and six elections to the House of Representatives further honed his skills.

Vermont's Republicans so esteemed Morrill, other candidates seldom opposed his renomination. In Vermont the Republican nomination was

equivalent to election. Between 1856, when the Republican Party partic-
ipated in its first national elections, and 1962, when Democrat William
Meyer became U.S. Representative, every Vermont senator, representative, governor and lieutenant governor was Republican. So Justin Morrill
had few challenges for office and little opportunity to show his political
expertise. When he decided to leave the House of Representatives and
seek election to the Senate in 1866 he did face significant opposition.
This campaign showed Morrill's political acumen at its finest.

The state legislature was not in session in November 1865 when
Senator Collamer died. Newly-elected Governor Paul Dillingham, therefore, would appoint a successor to serve until the 1866 election. Then the
state legislature would select someone for the full six-year term. William
Hebron, who had also been active in Vermont Whig politics, wrote
Morrill expressing the belief that whomever the governor appointed to
finish Collamer's term would have an unfair advantage in the 1866 election. Hebron suggested, therefore, that both Morrill and Poland withdraw from consideration for the short term appointment. Hebron offered
himself, a non-candidate for the 1866 election, to fill the short term and
asked Morrill to write Governor Dillingham supporting this position.
Morrill agreed and complied with Hebron's request for a supportive letter. He was sure the governor would "see at once" the "gross impropriety" of appointing a presumed candidate to finish Collamer's term.
Morrill also wrote E. P. Walton, editor of the Montpelier *Watchman*,
asking him to write an editorial expressing the same view. Governor
Dillingham, however, must not have "seen at once" the impropriety—he
appointed Poland to complete Collamer's term.[9] Supporter Crosby Miller
told Morrill that Poland now believed he had the "inside track" for election to fill the seat, but Miller was convinced "the reverse was true."[10]

Undismayed by Poland's appointment, Morrill relied on the grass-
roots' tactics he had used to win reelection to the House of
Representatives five times. He had cultivated friendships with Whig and
later Republican party leaders and members throughout the state. He
corresponded often with his friends, exchanging political and personal
information. Before every congressional election, Morrill wrote asking
his friends' advice on whether he should seek election. Besides Willard,
Morrill corresponded with several other people around the state evalu-
ating his chances for election to the Senate. S. M. Gleason of Montpelier
answered, "The universal expression is *very favorable* and there can be
no doubt of the result."[11] J. M. Orson, also of Montpelier, replied that

voters in his area believed "Mr. Morrill is as able a man as any man in the Senate now."[12] This networking and informal polling were extremely accurate and effective.

Justin Morrill also cultivated friendships with newspapermen. As mentioned earlier, General E. P. Walton, *The Montpelier Watchman's* editor, supported Morrill with editorials. Later, after the general's son became editor, *The Watchman* continued its relationship with Morrill. C. W. Willard's *The Green Mountain Freeman*, Luther O. Greene's *Vermont Standard*, D. L. Milliken's *Vermont Record and Farmer*, and Hiram Atkin's *Bellows Falls Argus* were just four more of the 54 newspapers that received copies of speeches, government documents, and the Washington *Globe* that carried all the Congressional proceedings. Morrill also wrote articles and occasional editorials that appeared in these papers. In return, the newspapers printed his speeches and articles, keeping his name before the voters, and wrote editorials supporting his election.[13]

Indeed, Morrill enjoyed a special relationship with the press. P. T. Drew, of the *Burlington Record*, even invited Morrill to "tell me at any time when you think I can say anything for the *cause*."[14] Willard, too, wrote, "I shall be pleased at any time to have you make any suggestion, respecting what you would like to have the Freeman do or say."[15] By skillfully using the press and his political network of friends and supporters, Morrill kept his name before the voters and his finger on their pulse.

Judge Harris' lessons in meticulous record-keeping showed in Morrill's political practices. He made notations on envelopes he received indicating when he answered the letter and often the gist of his answer. Sometimes, he kept a draft copy or an improvised shorthand version of his response for his own records. Also, he compiled voter lists for the state. Morrill maintained numerous ledgers with voters' names, addresses, occupations, party affiliations, and the publications he had sent them. He sent publications and speeches to any voter who requested them, no matter their political party. As with the voters, Morrill kept extensive records of newspapers, their locations, editors, and politics, and the documents and speeches that he had sent. He also supported forty Vermont libraries with speeches and government documents.[16]

Vermont voters generally agreed with Morrill's voting record and his stand on issues. When opponents said Morrill had gone against the government by opposing the national bank and paper as legal tender, his friend E. C. Redington countered that Morrill had acted as his "constituents required," adding, "When they talk of these things I talk to them of the Tariff and Reciprocity and they are mum."[17]

Morrill's constituents also appreciated his thrift. A former Senate page later recalled that Morrill was as "careful of the public property as if he had bought and paid for it out of his private purse."[18] For example, he continued using a quill pen long after other members had switched to metal tips. Pages would place a fresh pen on Morrill's desk every morning, he would use it through the day then lock it in his desk at night. At the end of the session, he transferred the pens to his committee room where he continued to use them for months instead of ordering new ones. Morrill also saved the red tape from his mail. His was the only committee room never to order tape.[19] Morrill also claimed he never spent any money in seeking election.[20]

Integrity was another quality Vermonters valued in Morrill. In response to a letter complimenting his personal integrity, he explained, "while I would not claim to be better than the average of mankind, . . . I have made it an inflexible rule since I first came here not to make or try to make money from my knowledge of what Congress was doing or likely to do."[21] When a wine distributor wrote telling him to expect a gift of four cases of California wines, Morrill thanked the sender, then explained he could not accept the wine as a gift. He continued, "If, however, you will send me a bill of the wine forwarded, at your usual price, I will take it, and at once remit the amount. Otherwise, it will be left at the Express Office subject to your order."[22]

Morrill also strongly disliked lobbyists. When Charles M. Bliss, a lobbyist for the Monument Association, sought Morrill's help, the senator declined, stating, "my opinion has long been fixed adversely to the employment of paid agents to push measures pending before Congress." Another time he remarked, "my prejudices against hired lobbyists is very strong."[23] Such practices won the approval from voters of both major parties and he seldom had more than nominal opposition, even from Democrats.

Although he enjoyed wide-spread, bi-partisan support during his years in the House, Morrill often seemed a reluctant candidate. In his 1858 acceptance speech he announced he planned to retire from public service after that term "to the not less attractive duties which cluster around a Vermont home." He did not wish to tire his constituency, he wanted to give other men an opportunity to serve, and both his business and his health needed his care. Although pressured by supporters, including Vermont Governor Erastus Fairbanks, "not to shirk further public service," he remained determined. Just before the district convention, a candidate for the nomination wrote Morrill that the convention would nominate him despite his announced intention unless he was present. So Morrill attended. Almost immediately, the convention nominated and unanimously elected him. When he rose and declined the nomination, members of the convention told him they would not accept his declination. So he was the Republican candidate for Congress in 1860.[24]

In 1863 Morrill again decided to retire from Congress at the end of his term. He wrote fellow-Congressman E. B. Washburne that he was "really weary" and wanted to stay at home. In April 1863 he publicly announced he would not seek reelection. He felt it was the voters' "privilege" and "duty" to elect a "fresh man." Schuyler Colfax, another close friend and colleague, urged Morrill to reconsider, explaining that Congress could not afford to lose his experience in "tariff and internal tax bills." Colfax considered it Morrill's national duty to continue, adding that he could justifiably retire after the war was over. Francis Daniels, a voter in the Second District, perhaps had the strongest argument when he told Morrill the voters had supported him when he wanted to be elected and "we want you now for our own sake." Morrill held to his stated intention telling a friend "I trust nobody takes me for an ass who declines an office when he really wants it." Again, however, the district convention "drafted" him as its candidate. He accepted the nomination explaining he recognized "the right of the country in time of war to the life even of any citizen." Morrill's efforts to avoid reelection were probably sincere, but political opponents called them ploys to garner support. In 1866, when Morrill again announced he would not be a candidate for the House of Representatives, he truly meant it. He would either become senator or he would return to private life.[25]

As Morrill busied himself arranging support through his friends and the newspapers, Judge Poland's camp was active, too. Although former governor Smith apologized to Morrill for supporting Poland and explained he had promised to do so three years earlier, he and his backers worked "like braves" to ensure Poland's election for the six-year term. A rumor circulated that Morrill, as a "large owner of factory stock," had written tariff legislation that favored wool manufacturers over wool growers. Morrill admitted he owned a "few shares" of woolen mill stock. But, he explained, he owned many more shares in cotton manufacturing, banking, and real estate, all of which Congress had heavily taxed. Also, he had always opposed a tax on wool. He proclaimed, "But all my little parcels when put together are not enough to bribe the judgment of any true hearted man." Still the charge persisted. Finally, he responded, "If there is any man in Vt. who believes if my interests in woolen stock was multiplied a thousand fold, that my judgment or course would be swerved a hair's breadth thereby, I do not wish his support."[26]

Smith and his associates apparently secured enough letters from legislators pledging support for Poland to cause Morrill concern. He told his friend G. G. Benedict, editor of the Burlington *Daily and Weekly Free Press*, while Morrill's friends were quietly "seeking an honest verdict," Smith and the others were "doing more than my friends may be aware of." Morrill asked if Benedict knew any "good men" who could quietly work to counteract Smith's efforts. He then suggested the press make a concerted effort, beginning about 1 May, to thwart Smith and Poland's plan. Morrill assured Benedict that he was not "over eager for advancement" and would not be unhappy to return to private life, "if the state can do better than to retain me longer in its service."[27]

A friend informed Morrill, "There is great danger that intriguing demagogues may triumph over candid freemen both on the east and west side of our state and the glory of Vermont depart for a long time from the U.S. Senate."[28] Efforts in Poland's behalf apparently concerned Morrill enough that he considered returning to Vermont in April, before the Congressional session ended. He told Luther Greene, of the *Vermont Standard*, "I shall be compelled to go home in April or May and then I should like to meet some of my editorial friends at some point."[29] He also wrote Benedict about meeting with him and a "few friends, though I hardly know how to bring it about." Then, interestingly for a man who claimed to never have spent anything to get elected, Morrill suggested, "I should like to pay all expenses for such a meeting either in Vt., Springfield, Mass., or in New York, but it may not be the best."[30] Apparently, the gathering never took place.

In late March 1866, the election became more complicated when Vermont's other senator, Solomon Foot, died. Morrill considered Foot's death a personal and a public loss. But he recognized that the second vacancy could cause problems for the Smith-Poland coalition. Smith also had aspirations, being senator reportedly was the "dream of his life." Morrill believed that now Poland and Smith's "interests were divergent." The coalition suffered another blow when Governor Dillingham appointed Poland's good friend George Edmunds to replace Foot. Smith had begged the governor to appoint someone else and pleaded with Edmunds not to take the position. Smith then suggested appointing Morrill to fill the term until the legislature met in the fall. Although he offered to support Morrill's election in the legislature, he and another ally had apparently agreed to "shove [Morrill] to one side to make a place for Mr. Smith or Mr. Woodbridge whichever might then be strongest." Smith's professed magnanimity did not sway Dillingham.[31]

Morrill's friends suggested that he exploit the rift among Poland's supporters by forming an alliance with Edmunds. They wanted Morrill to support Edmunds in return for his endorsing Morrill's candidacy. Willard wrote Edmunds "making various suggestions and asking him to consider whether he ought further to aid Judge Poland." Morrill declined to "make any compacts." His friends had already assured him that he would win against any combination. He wanted the best man on the west side to win. He acknowledged, though, that his backers would not "cordially support" anyone who actively opposed him.[32]

But he would help his supporters gain office. Morrill considered enlisting his friend and fellow Vermont Congressman Portas Baxter to help General Stannard win a Congressional seat. Morrill explained to Benedict "what I want to do is to bring about harmony of actions among friends. . . . Will not what I propose be best if it can be done? I shall quietly try."[33]

Despite the internal struggle between his friends, Poland had considerable strength. Morrill acknowledged Edmund's appointment would diminish ex-Governor Smith's interest in the election, "[b]ut it does not break the slate of the Governor, Smalley, and Poland." Poland still had Governor Dillingham's backing and most of Vermont's lawyers and railroad interests supported him. He also took advantage of his appointed senatorial office by mailing so many government publications to voters that he overwhelmed some post offices in Vermont. The mailings prompted one voter to comment, "Electioneering has commenced in earnest. The Judge has commenced sending the public documents in great quantities."[34]

Poland's camp was surely behind the rumor that Morrill's stock holdings influenced his tariff legislation. Then, apparently realizing that too many local Republican leaders still preferred Morrill, Poland switched tactics. He stressed Morrill's invaluable service in the House of Representatives and claimed Vermont and the nation could not afford to lose Morrill's experience from the House. Poland's perfect solution was to retain himself in the Senate and Morrill in the House. If staying in the House did not satisfy him, Poland thought Morrill might accept a foreign mission. Commenting on the suggestion, Morrill thought "Judge P's idea of a foreign mission was good! But when I go abroad as I hope to do I intend to go at my own expense."[35]

Although Foot's death brought new candidates into the race, they did not directly affect Morrill's bid to replace Collamer. Vermont had long held to the tradition that one senator would come from the eastern side of the mountains and one from the western side. Collamer, like Morrill, was from the eastern side. Morrill's race was still against Poland.

In 1866 state legislatures elected U.S. senators, so the period before county conventions selected candidates for the legislature would be the best time to discuss the merits of the senatorial candidates. Morrill invited Walton to Washington. The congressman wanted to "advice" with the editor on "the history of several measures started by me." Morrill wanted Walton to "set forth from time to time in a brief paragraph such merits as they might fairly be entitled to—which paragraphs, coming from you, would be likely to circulate through the Vt. press."[36]

Morrill explained his strategy to his friend C. W. Willard, "In due time I shall, of course, announce my purpose of declining absolutely another election from my district. I think this will be proper sometime in May. . . . The noise that I cannot be spared from the Dist. will then be silence."[37] Since Willard held a "vigorous pen," Morrill asked him to examine his and Poland's records and to do justice "to whatever success it may show." He assured Willard he did not want to be "puffed and spattered with undeserved praise." Morrill offered to furnish some appropriate speeches to help Willard with his writing. Also, he planned to publicly announce his candidacy for the Senate in May 1866 and simultaneously refuse to be a candidate for the House. Apparently, Willard convinced him to delay issuing his letter declining reelection until after he returned home from Washington in June.[38]

Confident of ultimate success, Morrill continued corresponding with his friends, especially those in the press. He believed the state's industrial class and "educated men," except lawyers, would vote for him. But he encouraged people to judge each candidate on his merits and offered to withdraw if someone else could better promote the honor of the state. He cautioned, however, "brass and assurance do not always indicate genius or talent. Proof of these can only be given by works." "Brass" referred to Judge Poland, who like to dress in the colonial style wearing a great blue coat with brass buttons. The attire earned him the nickname "Brass Buttons."[39]

Still Morrill cautioned his supporters to take nothing for granted and to be alert for the "adroitness" of Poland and his backers. Apparently the rumor about his woolen manufacturing stock influencing his tariff legislation resurfaced and gained some credence among the Windsor County's farmers. Morrill believed if people examined his record they would find he had always sympathized with "agriculturists." His tariff record showed he had done all he could for the wool growers and more than any other legislator. "I have always got wool better placed than it was when I took hold of it." He explained to his friend J. W. Colburn being elected to the Senate meant little compared to his good name. "[I]f after a service of 10–12 years I should have lost the confidence of my constituents it would cause me profound grief." Morrill believed his own disclaimers might seem self-serving and expressed confidence that Colburn would not allow Morrill's "name to suffer any injustice."[40]

These charges slowly died and Morrill's reputation and his friends' efforts and editorial support helped kill them. Edward Seymour of Vergennes assured him, "Truth crushed to earth will rise again." The wool-growers in western Vermont realized how much Morrill had done for them and that he had the "disposition" and the power to do more than anyone else could.[41]

By June 1866 Morrill was ready for his next move. He had quietly gathered support through his friends and the press, including some with national circulation. Horace Greeley's New York *Tribune* proclaimed Vermont should elect Morrill "because of what he has done and is able to do for his State and the Union."[42] The Springfield, Massachusetts *Republican* and the Boston *Journal* encouraged Morrill's election. Luther Greene, editor of the *Vermont Standard*, agreed with the Springfield *Republican* when it said Morrill "is our best present to Congress." The out-of-state endorsements, however, prompted Poland to complain that outside opinion was influencing Vermont's elections.[43]

Also, several more Vermont newspapers, which had waited for the right moment, announced for Morrill. One source lauded his character and attributed it to "the soundness of his reasoning, the clearness of his apprehension of the wants of the country, the fidelity and zeal of his labor, the persistency of his indomitable purpose, and the genial courtesy of his manners which have left him without a personal enemy in Congress."[44]

Newspaper support became so widespread opponents started a rumor that he had "bought off" the press. But this gained little credence. Morrill thanked the West Randolph *Eagle's* editor for disputing the allegations. He did not believed it necessary to reassure P. P. Ripley that "I am incapable of stooping to any improper agency to promote my political interests, or of purchasing support. If I did such a thing I should certainly deem myself unworthy of public office as well as of the public respect."[45]

County conventions to select legislative candidates began in June. Windsor and Windham Counties chose Morrill supporters at their conventions. Then, on 20 June, Morrill publicly thanked the Second District's voters for "the repeated honors" and notified them he would not be a candidate for reelection as representative. Poland backers' arguments for keeping Morrill in the House now seemed valid reasons for electing him to the Senate.[46]

When Orange County Republicans met a few days later they passed a resolution citing Morrill's "united industry, eminent ability, and fidelity to the best interests not only of Vermont but of our whole country." They restricted their state legislature nominees to voting only for him for senator. As other conventions met and elected legislators who would support Morrill, the outcome soon became obvious. Crosby Miller wrote Morrill on 24 July that the "senatorial question is virtually settled" and the district convention would soon meet to select a candidate to succeed him.[47]

By this time Poland realized he could not win. His supporters sought a compromise with Morrill. Morrill, however, refused any agreement or deal. He did not, however, forbid his backers from acting in his behalf. Apparently, Poland and Morrill's men reached an accord, Poland would withdraw from the senatorial race and Morrill's friends would support him as the Second District's candidate for the House. Morrill's friend Maine Congressman James G. Blaine congratulated him for the "arrangement," which would be "far better for [Morrill's] personal ease and for party harmony." On 23 October, the Vermont Legislature confirmed what everyone already knew by electing Morrill to the Senate "with substantial unanimity." He celebrated with a party, including "an ample and festive supper," for the Legislature and two or three hundred friends.[48]

Ironically, as with his election to the House, sadness came with the joy of his elevation to the Senate. In February 1867, his mother Mary died. She was seventy-nine and her health had gradually failed as she grew older. Although her death did not surprise her son, it saddened him and made his recent victory seem bitter-sweet.[49]

Meanwhile, as Morrill worked to move to the Senate, he still continued his duties in the House. On 7 May 1866, he reported the Internal Revenue Bill. Projected income and expenses showed a $75 million excess. Morrill proposed reducing taxes on sugar, salt, coal, manufacturing, incomes and raw materials. Explaining his reasoning, he said, "But now the duties of peace return, and we must simplify our laws, reduce the burdens of taxpayers so far as possible, and cheapen the cost of living."[50] These cuts would eliminate the excess revenue. Taxes on whiskey, malt liquors and luxury items would remain the same. Any faster reduction, he warned, could damage the national credit. Both Houses approved the tax bill with few alterations and President Andrew Johnson signed it on 13 July 1866.[51]

Morrill's estimate of the 1866 budget excess was too conservative. On 13 February 1867, he reported a second tax reduction bill. This measure eliminated all taxes on "salt, clothing, leather, pottery-ware, tinware, and cooperage of all sorts." He explained this would "so reduce the revenue that no large balance would remain in the treasury to tempt any one to disregard the wisdom of economy."[52] This second revenue reduction bill would eliminate another $75 million in taxes. It quickly passed both Houses and became law.

Morrill's war revenue program had balanced internal taxes and the tariff. As internal taxes rose, he fought to increase tariff rates to compensate. This, he claimed, allowed American manufacturers to compete on equal grounds with foreign competitors. Now, he sought an overall reduction in the tariff to counter-balance the tax cuts. The rates on raw wool, however, would increase. He also proposed to retain some of the best features of the repealed Canadian Reciprocity Treaty. The tariff on coal, therefore, would drop from $1.25 to $.50 per ton. Opposition from staunch protectionists and coal-producing regions condemned Morrill's 1866 attempt to lower the trade barriers. The Senate delayed consideration until the second session and finally passed a much-amended version on 1 February 1867. With barely a month left until the session ended, there was insufficient time for the House to dispose of all the amendments. Morrill failed, for the only time, to have a tariff bill enacted.[53]

Besides seeking to cut internal taxes and tariff rates, Morrill also wanted to reduce or "contract" greenbacks in circulation and resume specie payments. In December 1865, Treasury Secretary Hugh

McCulloch, who replaced Fessenden in March 1865, recommended to Congress that he be allowed to sell U.S. bonds and use the proceeds to gradually retire the greenbacks. Morrill strongly agreed with McCulloch's position and, on 21 February 1866, presented a loan bill that would allow the treasury secretary to retire greenbacks "as fast as a sound economy will permit." Inflationists, led by Thaddeus Stevens, objected to giving the secretary so much power. Eventually, the two sides compromised. The law, passed in April 1866, authorized the secretary to withdraw $10 million in greenbacks within the next six months and no more than $4 million in any month thereafter.[54]

In addition to financial issues, reconstructing the former Confederate states and readmitting their representatives to Congress occupied much of the Thirty-ninth Congress. Immediately after the new Congress organized, Thaddeus Stevens proposed a resolution creating a joint committee to consider conditions in the former Confederate states and report whether any were entitled to resume their places in Congress. Stevens further suggested that neither House allow a southern member to assume his seat until the committee submitted its report. The committee's final report cited continued southern abuses of the newly freed African-Americans and recommended that only Tennessee be immediately readmitted. Congressional reaction to this report formed the basis for the Fourteenth Amendment to the Constitution. The amendment defined citizens as "all persons born or naturalized in the United States," forbade states from depriving citizens of "life, liberty or property, without due process of law," reduced federal representation for states withholding voting rights from male citizens, and dictated the terms under which former Confederates could serve in federal positions. Morrill served on this Joint Committee of Fifteen, or the Joint Committee on Reconstruction as it is sometimes known; but, his Ways and Means' duties kept him from an active role. He did agree with the committee's actions and signed the final report.[55]

The Thirty-ninth Congress adjourned on 3 March 1867. The next day the Fortieth Congress convened, the first for Senator Morrill. After his election to the Senate, Morrill's attitude toward politics seemed to change. Although he offered not to stand for reelection if Vermont's voters had someone else they preferred, he never again publicly mentioned retiring. Also, as a fiscally conservative Republican from a staunchly conservative Republican state, Morrill must have begun to feel some job security in the Senate. His friend Blaine assured him,

"You can now 'set your house in order' for a twelve year service in the Senate, at least."[56]

Senator Justin Morrill became more comfortable in Washington. Some years later he declined a cabinet appointment preferring to stay in the Senate. He explained, "There is no gift, no office to which I could be appointed, that I would accept in preference to a seat in the United States Senate. I consider that the highest honor that could be bestowed on me, and [its duties] the highest function that I could perform."[57] He carried many issues with him from the House to the Senate. The struggle to shrink greenbacks in circulation and resume specie payments continued. Also, the disagreement between President Johnson and Radical Republicans in Congress over southern reconstruction threatened to erupt into political warfare.

Notes

1. Wright to Judge M. L. Bennett, 9 April 1866, LOC.
2. Hoyer, "Gentleman from Vermont," 210–16.
3. Parker, *Morrill*, 171.
4. Ibid.
5. Morrill to unknown addressee, ca. 1865, LOC.
6. Morrill to C. W. Willard, 10 November 1865, LOC.
7. Ibid.
8. J. M. Orson to Morrill, 31 October 1865, LOC.
9. Wm. Hebron to Morrill, 10 November 1865; Morrill to Dillingham, n.d., LOC.
10. Miller to Morrill, 24 November 1865, LOC.
11. Gleason to Morrill, 27 October 1865, LOC.
12. Orson to Morrill, 31 October 1865, LOC.
13. See Morrill Collection in LOC.
14. P. T. Drew to Morrill, 24 May 1866, LOC.
15. Willard to Morrill, 13 February 1866, LOC.
16. The Morrill Collection, Library of Congress, has most of his correspondence and many of his political ledgers.
17. Redington to Morrill, 7 November 1865, LOC.
18. *Burlington Free Press and Times*, 27 January 1899, LOC.
19. Ibid.
20. Morrill interview with unnamed Washington newspaper, LOC.
21. Morrill to Calvin Blodgett, 8 February 1873, Cornell University Library.
22. Morrill to Perkins, Stone and Co., 18 December 1865, LOC.
23. Morrill to Bliss, 21 August 1891 and 4 October 1892.
24. Morrill's 1858 acceptance speech; Morrill to Jonathan Ross, 21 March 1896, LOC.
25. Morrill to E. B. Washburne, 6 January 1863; Morrill to "The Voters of the Second Congressional District," 27 April 1863; Morrill to Col. G. W. Merrill, 24 June 1863,

LOC; Francis Daniels to Morrill, 28 February 1863, Morrill Collection, Vermont Historical Society; Schuyler Colfax to Morrill, 2 May 1863; Morrill's Acceptance Speech, delivered at White River Junction, 21 July 1863, Morrill Collection, Cornell University.

26. Crosby Miller to Morrill, 26 February 1866; Morrill to Crosby Miller, 28 February 1866; Morrill to G. G. Benedict, 19 March 1866; Morrill to Edward Seymour, 9 April 1866, LOC.

27. Morrill to G. G. Benedict, 19 March 1866; Morrill to Horace E. Royce, 19 March 1866, LOC.

28. E. Seymour to Morrill, 3 April 1866, LOC.

29. Morrill to Greene, 19 March 1866, LOC.

30. Morrill to Benedict, 19 March 1866, LOC.

31. Ibid.

32. I. T. Drew to Morrill, 4 April 1866; C. W. Willard to Morrill, 5 April 1866; Morrill to Willard, 7 April 1866; Morrill to H. H. Henry, 9 April 1866, LOC.

33. Morrill to Benedict, 31 March 1866, LOC.

34. E. C. Redington to Morrill, 3 April 1866, LOC.

35. Luther Greene to J. W. Colburn, n.d.; Crosby Miller to Morrill, 26 February 1866; E. C. Redington to Morrill, 3 April 1866; E. Seymour to Morrill, 3 April 1866; Morrill to H. H. Henry, 9 April 1866; Morrill to E. P. Walton, 7 April 1866, LOC; Parker, *Morrill*, 172–73.

36. Morrill to Walton, 31 March 1866, LOC.

37. Morrill to C. W. Willard, 30 March 1866, LOC.

38. Ibid.; Willard to Morrill, 4 April 1866, LOC.

39. Morrill to G. G. Benedict, 9 April 1866; Morrill to Thomas McDaniels, 12 April 1866; Morrill to D. B. Dudley, 19 April 1866, LOC; Parker, *Morrill*, 172.

40. Morrill to Milo Bennett, 9 April 1866; Morrill to J. W. Colburn, 21 April 1866, LOC.

41. E. Seymour to Morrill, 15 May 1866, LOC.

42. Reprinted in Benedict's *Free Press*, 25 May 1866.

43. Parker, *Morrill*, 173; Greene to J. W. Colburn, n.d., LOC.

44. Parker, *Morrill*, 175.

45. Morrill to Ripley, 13 July 1866, LOC.

46. J. T. Drew to Morrill, 12 June 1866; James G. French to Morrill, 20 June 1866; Dan L. Milliken to Morrill, 20 June 1866; draft made by Dr. B. Dudley (at Morrill's request) to The Electors of the Second Congressional District of Vermont, 20 June 1866; Morrill to P. P. Ripley, 13 July 1866, LOC.

47. E. M. Snyder to Morrill, 26 June 1866; Crosby Miller to Morrill, 24 July 1866, LOC.

48. Crosby Miller to Morrill, 24 July 1866; James G. Blaine to Morrill, 19 August 1866, LOC; Parker, *Morrill*, 174. Poland was elected to the House and served notably for several years. Also, Edmunds had a distinguished career in the Senate.

49. Parker, *Morrill*, 184.

50. Ibid., 166–67.

51. Hoyer, "Gentleman from Vermont," 216–18.

52. Ibid., 233–34.

53. Ibid., 226–27; Stanwood, *American Tariff Controversies*, 146–50.

54. See Chapter Seven for a more thorough discussion of Morrill's opposition to the green-backs. Morrill, speech, "The Loan Bill,", delivered in the House of Representatives, 21

February 1866, LOC; Hugh McCulloch, *Men and Measures of Half a Century* (New York: Charles Scribner's Sons, 1900), 210–11; Robert P. Sharkey, *Money, Class, and Party: An Economic Study of Civil War and Reconstruction* (Baltimore: Johns Hopkins Press, 1959), 60–74; Hoyer, "Gentleman from Vermont," 236–39.

55. Francis Fessenden, *Life and Public Services of William Pitt Fessenden* (Boston: Houghton, Mifflin and Company, 1907), 2: 14–199. Hoyer, "Gentleman from Vermont," 211–15; Eric Foner, *Reconstruction: America's Unfinished Revolution, 1863–1877* (New York: Harper and Row, Publishers, 1988), 239–60.

56. Blaine to Morrill, 19 August 1866, LOC.

57. *Burlington Free Press and Times,* April 1897.

7

SENATOR MORRILL

We have just emerged from a most expensive war, and ought to exhibit that spirit which success justly inspires, grappling with the financial difficulties remaining as part of our inheritance with the courage that conquers, and thus secure the vital interests of our own people while we challenge the respect of foreign nations.[1]

Justin Morrill

Although Morrill authored his most memorable legislation in the House, he made important contributions in the Senate. Helping to restore the nation's currency to a sound basis was perhaps his most significant effort. As Morrill's tenure in Congress grew, so did his reputation. Eventually he became one of the most esteemed and powerful members of Congress. Initially, however, his Senate duties were light and allowed him time to fulfill a lifelong dream.

As chair of the House Ways and Means Committee, he had maintained a full and busy schedule. As a new member of the Senate Finance Committee, he had few responsibilities or duties. He decided, therefore, to take a long awaited trip to Europe. Ruth apparently did not feel well enough to travel, so he invited fellow Vermonter and congressman E. L. Woodbridge and Maine Congressman James G. Blaine to accompany him. Woodbridge begged off, explaining House duties prevented him from going. Armed with letters of introduction to businessmen, politicians, and diplomats in England, France, the Netherlands, and Italy, Morrill and Blaine sailed aboard the *China* about 20 May 1867.[2]

They stopped first in Ireland. Twenty years later, Morrill would recall the "marvelous . . . first view of the beauty of the Emerald Isle," the Irish dog-carts and the Blarney stone.[3] The antiquity of the Irish cathedrals and castles filled him with "awe and wonder." He wrote Louise that America was so new he could hardly believe he was seeing buildings constructed in the fifth century. But the deterioration of the older buildings showed "[t]he genius and labor of the weightiest men at last turns to dust. God alone is eternal."[4]

In London Charles Francis Adams, the American minister, invited them to dinner. The next day he had the legation secretary escort them to Parliament and help them gain admission to the floor of the House of Commons. After meeting several members of Parliament, including William E. Forster and John Stuart Mill, Morrill and Blaine were invited to sit on the Peers' Bench, a position of honor. The two Americans then moved to the House of Lords and again received seats on the floor. Both men thoroughly enjoyed the experience.[5]

English railroads and roads impressed Morrill. Trains sped along at thirty miles per hour, with the expresses averaging forty miles per hour or more. The faster trains were "said to meet with the fewest accidents. But it is a fearful rate to ride." He preferred a carriage on the "Macadamized" British roads that made "a ride everywhere enjoyable."[6]

While in England, Morrill and Blaine also visited Kenilworth, Stratford-on-Avon, and Oxford. Morrill described the area in great detail in a letter to Ruth. He wrote of Kenilworth's ivy-covered ruins, with marble fireplaces and oaken ceilings. "The whole view or any part would make up such views as the schools love to paint."[7] At Stratford-on-Avon the Americans saw not only the house "but the very room where Will Shakespeare was born." Morrill especially admired Oxford and the university's twenty colleges. He remarked he would like to "lead Jimmy through these old halls a few years hence and tell him that very probably all the education he could get in an ordinary American college would hardly do more than fit him to enter here."[8]

Morrill marveled at Kew's "conservatories, lawns, trees, beds of flowers," and called it "the finest place I have ever seen." He admitted the "massive beds of Rhododendrons" surpassed his own in "extent and beauty," even though one "old lady" had traveled all the way from North Randolph to see his. The country gardens so impressed Morrill, he felt he "could write some pages about this day's sight-seeing." Blaine and Morrill also attended the races at Hyde Park, where the Prince of Wales evidently identified the two Americans by their "round soft hats," for "here no one wears such shocking bad hats."[9] Despite his obvious appreciation for England Morrill did not form a flattering opinion of the English people, whom he described as "not an agreeable people, . . . rather independent than polite—cold, not sympathizing easily with strangers—brutal rather than kindly."[10]

From England the travelers sailed for France, then on to Belgium and the Netherlands. Upon landing in Calais, France, "the bare-legged, dirty fish-women on the pier was the first foreignish sight which struck us." Morrill felt helpless at his inability to converse in French and having to resort to "little better than pantomime" to make himself understood. In Holland Morrill noticed bareheaded, barelegged women working in the fields "in the coarsest kind of drudgery." He commented, "Here is a field for the laborers in behalf of women's rights."[11]

As they sailed up Germany's Rhine Valley, Morrill marveled at the terraced vineyards along the steep shores. Again the age of castles, cathedrals, and towns fascinated him. "[T]hese old houses which have stood from the ninth, tenth, twelfth, and fifteenth century are more matters of wonder to me, from a country where we nearly all know the first settler in every town."[12] His visit to Hamburg, however, made the greatest impression and caused him to question German morals. On Sunday, "when church bells should be calling the people together for the holiest of thoughts," a band of musicians entertained a "miscellaneous throng" with marches, waltzes, and operas—"all executed with marvelous skill, to be sure, but all to toll the thoughtless and giddy as well as the already wrecked in morals into the very jaws of hell." He admitted many people came to Hamburg to enjoy the mineral springs, but the gambling tables attracted the largest crowd. To see well-dressed women among the patrons "was revolting to all [his] sensibilities." He thanked God there was no such "hell" in America. But despite such aversion, he wanted to examine this hell, so that he might "have a correct idea of the game, its *modus operandi* and all its accessories. Of course, such vices as the women of Babylon practiced [were] not unknown" in Hamburg. "Is it not too bad that a place beautiful by nature, and made attractive by the expenditure of vast wealth and taste, should be prostituted to such unholy purposes?" he mused.[13]

Although Morrill thoroughly enjoyed his trip, he also missed his family. He wrote Ruth from Venice of his disappointment at not receiving letters from her. "Since the days of courtship I have not looked forward for letters more anxiously." He believed the "parties to whom [he] had entrusted [his] correspondence" were at fault. He asked her to continue writing and assured her he would get the letters "ere long."[14]

After Italy, Morrill and Blaine visited Paris, "a wonderful city in extent, in wonders and manners," including Napoleon's Tomb, the Tuileries, the Louvre, Fontainebleu, and Versailles. The Emperor Napoleon III's stable under the Louvre especially appealed to Morrill. "The cleanliness of the stables was such that a blind man would not know in passing through them the use of the building, and the hair of the horses shone as bright as the silkiest of velvets."[15]

Morrill and Blaine then returned to England. Lingering in London for about two weeks, they again visited Westminster Abbey, Windsor Castle, and of course, Parliament. After listening to several members of the House of Lords debate a reform bill, Morrill concluded that none was the equal of "[William] Fessenden, [Charles] Sumner, [Lyman] Trumbull, [Andrew] Johnson, [John] Sherman, or even several other among our Senators." He later observed the American Congress had more "good debaters," but members of Parliament were "certainly more orderly and decorous in their behavior."[16] Morrill also attended the Goodwood races at Chichester, where "at one time eight horses together, flying like the wind, with the little jockies [sic] on them in the gayest costumes, made [his] blood tingle and [his] heart go pitty-pat."[17] Then, after a short visit to Scotland, the two travelers returned home about 1 September. Blaine later recalled, as they sailed into New York that both agreed they could have chosen no better traveling companion.[18]

Upon his return, Morrill confronted the impending impeachment of Pres. Andrew Johnson. He had followed the conflict between Johnson and the Radical Republicans in the newspapers in Europe. In June he had expressed to Ruth his alarm that Congress would act to impeach Johnson while Morrill was away. If that happened he feared the Democrats would "very likely" win the next presidential election. He added, "The country cannot afford that, whatever the demerits of Johnson."[19]

Congress did meet for an extra session before Morrill returned from Europe, but took no action against the president. Johnson and Radical Republicans were headed for their own "irrepressible conflict" even before Morrill left the House of Representatives. Before Lincoln's death, the Radicals had fought him for control of reconstruction in the South. Lincoln had offered the states most generous terms—if a state approved the Thirteenth Amendment ending slavery and 10 percent of its 1860 voters pledged support for the federal Constitution, he would consider the state reconstructed. The Radicals countered with the Wade-Davis Bill, which required a majority of voters to take the oath, banned those who would not from voting, barred Confederate leaders from ever holding office, and guaranteed freedmen equality before the law. Lincoln vetoed the measure. After his reelection, Lincoln had the political backing to enact his policies, in spite of Radical Republican opposition.

Johnson, selected as Lincoln's running mate to help secure the Border State vote, had neither his predecessor's political acumen nor his popularity. Immediately after his ascension to the presidency, the Radicals believed Johnson agreed with their plan for reconstruction. Instead, he pursued Lincoln's lenient course. This action cost the life-long Democrat and southerner any semblance of Radical support. The thin veneer of cooperation quickly gave way to confrontation, then to open hostility.

Testimony before the Joint Committee on Reconstruction[20] showed that the "reconstructed" states had enacted Black Codes that virtually reenslaved southern blacks. In response to this, in February 1866, therefore, Congress extended the Freedmen's Bureau, a wartime agency that helped former slaves. The following month both houses approved a bill to "protect all persons in the United States in their civil rights." The president vetoed both measures, but the Radical-led Congress overrode the vetoes.[21]

Johnson denounced the Reconstruction Committee as "an irresponsible central directory" and accused it of usurping the powers of government. In a Washington's Birthday speech, he labeled Thaddeus Stevens, Charles Sumner, and Wendell Phillips as traitors saying they opposed restoring the southern states to the Union. The president even hinted that the Radicals meant to assassinate him. The final break came after Johnson denounced the Fourteenth Amendment[22] and counseled southern states not to ratify it.[23]

Determined to take his case to the people, the president made a "swing around the circle" traveling as far west as St. Louis. He felt confident the voters would support his position and replace the Radicals in Congress in the upcoming election. Johnson's speeches, described as "rambling, vulgar, vindictive, and loaded with self-pity," had the opposite effect. The Republicans won control of every northern state legislature, every contested northern gubernatorial seat, and a two-thirds majority in both houses of Congress.[24]

When the Thirty-ninth Congress met for its last session, in December 1866, it left little doubt it would try to reduce the extraordinary powers the president had assumed during the Civil War. First, Congress claimed the right to call itself into special session. Previously, only the president had exercised that power. The Radicals were not going to give Johnson free rein from March until December, when Congress would have normally begun the new session.[25]

Next, the Radicals added a rider to the Army Appropriation Act restricting the president's power as commander in chief. From then on, he and the secretary of war could only issue military orders through the "General of the Army" (the assumed Republican presidential nominee for 1868, U.S. Grant). Congress then seized control of patronage by passing the Tenure of Office Act. If a presidential appointee required Senate approval, the president could not remove the appointee without Senate consent. The law specifically prohibited the president, without Senate concurrence, from replacing a cabinet officer he had appointed. The Radicals intended to protect Secretary of War Edwin Stanton who sympathized with their cause.[26]

Finally, the House adopted a resolution by Ohio representative James M. Ashley instructing the Judiciary Committee to investigate the president's conduct. Ashley charged that Johnson had abused his veto power, illegally returned rebel property, pardoned known traitors, and been involved in Lincoln's assassination. After a thorough investigation, the committee voted five to four not to recommend impeachment. The committee reversed itself in December, however, after Johnson asserted he would "stand on his rights, regardless of the consequences." But on 7 December 1867, the House rejected the committee's recommendation by a 57 to 108 vote.[27]

Meanwhile, in August 1867, Johnson had removed Stanton while Congress was not in session. Following the letter of the Tenure of Office Act, he appointed Grant as interim secretary pending congressional approval. When Congress convened in December, it refused to approve Stanton's removal. Much to Johnson's chagrin, Grant then withdrew in favor of Stanton. But the 7 December House vote to reject impeachment apparently emboldened Johnson. He decided to reassert his presidential powers and perhaps endear himself to the Democrats as their potential 1868 presidential nominee. Johnson dismissed Stanton and appointed Gen. Lorenzo Thomas in his stead, in apparent violation of the Tenure of Office Act. Stanton, encouraged by the Radicals, refused to leave his office and, instead, barricaded himself in. The Radical-led House of Representatives retaliated against President Johnson on 28 February 1868, by voting 126 to 47 to impeach him for "high crimes and misdemeanors in office."[28]

When the trial began on 5 March 1868, House impeachment managers[29] claimed, although Johnson was guilty of "high crimes and misdemeanors," that the impeachment procedure was a political rather than a judicial process. Under this reasoning, the Senate would only have to decide if Johnson was fit to retain his office, not whether he was guilty of a crime. Chief Justice Salmon Chase, who was presiding, disagreed and ruled the Senate must act as a court and all the rules of jurisprudence applied. The impeachment managers presented eleven articles or charges. The first eight related to Stanton's removal. Number nine accused Johnson of violating the Army Appropriation Act. Number ten said the president had been "unmindful" of his duties and had attempted to bring Congress into "disgrace, ridicule, hatred, contempt and reproach." Article eleven repeated all the previous charges and added that the president, in saying Congress represented "only a part of the United States," had questioned the legality of congressional actions.[30]

Because of the illness of Thaddeus Stevens, Benjamin Butler acted as the chief "prosecutor" in the impeachment trial. Chase's ruling forced the impeachment managers to focus on article eleven. This weakened their case because there was some doubt that the law applied to Stanton. Lincoln, not Johnson, had appointed him. But the defense had its own problems. Johnson's defense team, led by William Evarts, argued first that the president had obeyed the Tenure of Office Act, then it claimed Johnson purposely violated the law to test its validity in the Supreme Court.[31]

Justin Morrill, though a House member of the Reconstruction Committee and a supporter of the Radicals' position,[32] had his doubts about the wisdom of impeachment. He did believe, however, that Johnson was trying to undo the northern victory. "Our martial heroes triumphed and utterly vanquished rebellion in the field," he wrote. "Now, shall a civilian—not having miraculous virtues certainly—command, galvanize and nurse the monster again to life?" He felt Johnson's reconstruction policies had created "a crisis so grave it defie[d] exaggeration." But instead of impeachment, Morrill preferred tying Johnson's hands through restrictive legislation.[33] Just before the Senate voted on Johnson's guilt or innocence, Morrill wrote his friend William Fessenden,

"Not much in favor of [the Tenure of Office Act] nor of impeachment as original questions, yet I must do my duty." He then added, "I hope my judgment is not warped by political considerations."[34]

The Senate decided to consider article eleven first. A conviction required a two-thirds majority or thirty-six senators. Everyone believed the vote would be close. In his letter to Fessenden, Morrill wanted his friend to be "right on the constitutional and legal questions involved." He then assured him they would remain friends no matter which way Fessenden voted. But Morrill expressed concern that Fessenden might cast a vote that would damage his reputation and tear "your life out of you for the rest of your days." He then cautioned Fessenden, "You cannot afford to be buried with Andrew Johnson" adding, "nor can a poor devil like myself afford to have a cloud of suspicion thrown on the correctness of his vote by a wholly different vote given by yourself on a question of so grave consequences as that pending." Morrill concluded, "All I desire in the present issue is justice to the President and to our country."[35]

On 16 May 1867, thirty-five senators, including Justin Morrill, voted guilty. Nineteen, including Fessenden, voted not guilty. The Senate failed by one vote to convict President Johnson. Historian Eric Foner points out, however, that several other senators stood ready to vote for acquittal if needed. Morrill, in explaining his vote, acknowledged Johnson had taken "a bold, outspoken stand in behalf of the Union." But his appointment of corrupt men, "discreditable use of pardoning power," veiled threats to forcibly oppose what he called "an unconstitutional act of Congress," and "malign attempts to foist upon the country his policy of restoring the rebellious States" impelled Morrill to vote for conviction.[36]

In truth, however, Morrill probably did let "political consideration" warp his judgment. He loved the Republican Party and considered it the nation's savior. "A longer life to the Republican Party," he would later write, "seems to me essential in order that its works . . . may harden into the very bones of the Constitution."[37] In addition, his constituents vehemently backed the impeachment and urged Morrill to kick out "our accidental excellency."[38] Fessenden took the higher road. Explaining his vote, he wrote simply, "The agony is over . . . it is enough to say that I could come to no other conclusion, and not for all this world could I violate my oath to party mandates."[39]

Despite Morrill's earlier concerns, the Republicans carried the 1868 election. With Ulysses S. Grant's election, peace returned to

Washington and the Republican Party. Although Morrill strongly supported Grant, he retained his right to disagree with policies he deemed harmful to the country or to Vermont. He opposed the president's plan to annex Santo Domingo as he would later object to the annexation of Cuba and Hawaii. Morrill's reasons for opposing these acquisitions, while supporting Canada's incorporation into the United States, are unclear. In an article in *Forum* magazine he wrote, "I have long supposed that a political union of Canada with the United States might be only a question of time."[40] But when faced with the possibility of adding more Mexican territory, he believed that might give "us more of the Latin race than the stomach of Uncle Sam can safely bear."[41] Perhaps he, like many others of his generation, objected because he considered the people of color in Santo Domingo, Cuba, and Hawaii to be unfit for U.S. citizenship.

Morrill also stood against the majority of his party when he opposed the seating of two Republican senators who won office through devious means. Joseph C. Abbott of North Carolina had overwhelmingly lost to a Confederate Civil War veteran, who was later disqualified from holding office. Alexander Caldwell of Kansas had paid his Democratic opponent $15,000 to withdraw from the race. Morrill also angrily attacked Grant's friend and secretary of war, W. W. Belknap, who resigned the same day the House of Representatives unanimously voted to impeach him for corruption. In a Senate speech Morrill charged, "And thus the great remedy of impeachment 'for treason, bribery, and other high crimes and misdemeanors' of all United States civil officers . . . would be torn out by the roots and thrown like a worthless weed away."[42] Although he attacked Grant's policies and sometimes his friends, Morrill "made no assault on the President."[43]

As a leading Republican, Morrill also assumed the role of mediator between President Grant and two other powerful Republicans—Charles Sumner and Horace Greeley. Senate Foreign Relations chair Sumner led the successful fight against the president's proposal to annex Santo Domingo. Immediately after the Senate rejected the annexation, Grant fired Sumner's friend John Motley as minister to England. Sumner took the firing as a personal attack and strongly criticized the president. Morrill tried to intercede. He spoke with Grant, who convinced him Motley's removal was not connected to Sumner's stand on Santo Domingo. Morrill then wrote Sumner assuring him that the president meant no affront to him and reminding him that Grant was the

Republican Party leader and the "first man of the nation." Sumner was not to be persuaded. Morrill even asked Secretary of State Hamilton Fish to intercede. Fish "made the earnest effort to convince and to conciliate Mr. Sumner, but . . . he was not in the mood and *would* not be convinced." Sumner continued his harsh attacks on Grant. Morrill again appealed to Sumner to cease his presidential name-calling. But Morrill's words could not soothe Sumner's wounded ego. He continued his tirade and, in the next congressional session, Senate leaders removed him as Foreign Relations Committee chair.[44]

Like Sumner, Horace Greeley was a Republican Party leader with a fragile ego. Using his influential New York *Tribune* as a forum, Greeley criticized Grant and the Republican Party in 1872. Morrill wrote Greeley saying he was a "life subscriber" of the *Tribune*, but the paper's recent attitude bothered him. He asked Greeley to work within the party to correct its problems instead of attacking the party and the president. Morrill explained, "I care not how fiercely any rascality is assailed; but surely the whole Republican Party has not suddenly become rotten."[45] He cautioned the venerable editor that continued attacks would threaten his position as a Republican leader.

Greeley, like Sumner, was not to be appeased. He replied, "I forgive the ignorant who talk as you do; I hold such as you responsible for misleading them. The man who could make such cabinets as Grant has had is hardly fit for a justice of the peace."[46] Greeley left the Republican Party to oppose Grant as the Liberal Republican and Democratic Party candidate in the 1872 election. After his overwhelming defeat, he died within a month. Morrill succeeded with neither Republican dissident, but his role reflected his respected position within the party.

Morrill generated some controversy of his own in 1873. During the 1872–73 winter session, Congress raised members' salaries from $5,000 to $7,500 a year and made the pay raise retroactive for two years. Morrill consistently and vigorously opposed the bill, but it passed anyway. The irate public quickly dubbed the measure the "Salary Grab" Act. When Morrill received his "back pay," he forwarded the $4,300 check to the Vermont treasurer, stating, "Having at every stage, by vote, speech and question of order, done what I could, though ineffectually, to defeat the recent legislation touching the pay of members of Congress, I feel that I shall best consult my own self respect by emptying my pockets of this back pay. . . ."[47] Surprisingly, criticism that he should have turned the money over to the federal treasury instead generated such a reaction

Morrill felt the need to explain himself. In his "Public Letter" printed in the Burlington *Free Press and Times*, he told his constituents,

> my purpose not to receive the "back pay" was avowed, and the only matter undetermined was what should be done with it, and this at last was determined in accordance with what to me appeared to be the simple dictate of duty, and the sternest requirements of equity. Being able to trace so much of it, I restored it to those from whence it came.[48]

Apparently, this did not quiet his political opponents immediately, but the controversy eventually subsided. The integrity Morrill showed in the "Salary Grab" carried over to the Finance Committee where he did perhaps his most important work in the Senate.

Unlike his years in the House, Morrill broke little new ground in the Senate. As biographer William Parker said, "He had worked out the articles of his political creed, and was content to abide by them."[49] Upon Morrill's election to the Senate, Fessenden, who had returned to the Finance Committee chair, wrote Morrill, "I congratulate you somewhat, and myself more." Fessenden intended for Morrill to serve on his committee.[50] Morrill remained on the Finance Committee for the rest of his career, first as a member and then as chair. As mentioned earlier, he continued to fight to maintain moderate protection.[51] Probably his greatest contribution in the Senate was his attempt to restore a sound currency following the helter-skelter efforts to finance the Civil War.

A fiscal conservative, Morrill had opposed the issuance of greenbacks and advocated a strong, stable currency backed by gold. He also believed the nation's credit depended upon resuming the practice of redeeming federal notes with gold (specie) as quickly as possible. Hugh McCulloch, who replaced Fessenden as treasury secretary, held similar views. Before coming to the Treasury, McCulloch had been a successful banker, served as comptroller of currency, and had established the national banking system. To the secretary, the legal-tender acts were emergency war measures. Now that the emergency had passed, the greenbacks should be quickly retired. Before Morrill moved from the House, he sponsored a bill incorporating McCulloch's recommendations (which coincided with his own).[52]

On 21 February 1866, Morrill reported the bill extending the treasury secretary's authority and authorizing him to fund non-interest bearing portions of the public debt (greenbacks). Essentially, the bill was approving what McCulloch had already begun. Since 1 July 1865, he had removed $25 million in greenbacks from circulation. Morrill wanted Congress to sanction the action and to give the secretary authority to retire the greenbacks at the rate and time he thought best. Morrill told Congress, "The simple question is, will you perpetuate this war-made expansion of the currency and all its illimitable brood of evils, or will you authorize a financier, who shows himself competent to the task, to retire the excess as fast as sound economy will permit?"[53]

Strong voices, including Samuel Hopper, William D. Kelley, Calvin T. Hulburd, James A. Garfield, and Thaddeus Stevens, opposed the bill. Some members wanted to return to specie payment, but not reduce the greenbacks in circulation. Others believed accumulating a large gold reserve would raise the value of greenbacks and eliminate the need to retire them. Another group wanted to wait for industry and finance to adjust themselves before acting. Westerners opposed any contraction of paper money. These various factions combined to defeat Morrill's bill by a seventy to sixty-five vote, with forty-nine members abstaining.[54]

New York congressman Roscoe Conkling convinced the House to recommit the bill to committee for revision. On 23 March 1866, Morrill reported a revised version limiting the secretary to retiring no more than $10 million in greenbacks within the first six months after the bill's passage. Then he could retire no more than $4 million per month. This new version passed eighty-three to forty-three, with forty-seven members abstaining. President Johnson signed it on 12 April 1866. McCulloch predicted he would resume specie payments by 1 July 1868.[55]

Conditions rendered McCulloch's (and Morrill's) optimism premature. In May 1866, the great Overend-Gurney stock crash in London's Lombard Street sent the Bank of England's discount rate to 10 percent. Within two weeks, more than $20 million in gold flowed from the United States to England, and more followed. Between April and June gold premiums climbed from 127 to 167 and stayed there until November. A poor grain crop, Indian wars, the cost of military governments in the South, and other unexpected expenses also drained gold. The gold crisis affected the U.S. economy, especially western farmers. Morrill favored raising the value of legal-tender notes to be on par with gold currency, then withdrawing them beginning in 1869. Opponents disagreed with this plan and blamed McCulloch's contraction of currency for the financial hardships. Congress passed a bill suspending further reductions. President Johnson refused to sign it, but instead of vetoing the measure, he allowed it to become law, on 4 February 1868, without his signature. McCulloch's (and Morrill's) plan of gradual contraction of greenbacks in circulation was dead. In its two years of operation, the secretary retired $44 million in greenbacks. Morrill had lost this round, but he would continue to fight.[56]

When Grant became president, George S. Boutwell replaced McCulloch as treasury secretary. Boutwell concentrated on refunding the public debt at a lower interest rate and largely ignored the greenbacks. Morrill agreed with refinancing the public debt, but recommended other measures, too. To him, sound currency was not only good fiscal policy, it was a matter of national integrity. The federal government had taken emergency measures to finance the war. Now that the war was over, the nation should operate on solid financial principles. In March 1868, he spoke against a funding bill sponsored by Finance Committee chair John Sherman, who assumed the chair after Fessenden died. Morrill opposed the bill because it reduced the interest rate on bonds, made the new bonds interchangeable with greenbacks, and would reissue the $44 million in greenbacks that McCulloch has just withdrawn from circulation. Convinced that continued withdrawal was necessary for a sound money policy, Morrill explained, "Not believing . . . that the way out of a sea of troubles is to wade further in, I cannot give my vote in that direction. . . ."[57] Instead, he urged the government to reduce expenses to the "lowest reasonable point, such as will compel every department to live from hand to mouth." Morrill believed that Congress should decrease taxes proportionately; that gold and silver coin should be restored as circulating currency; that the national banking system should be extended to "accommodate all parts of the country"; and, that the treasury secretary should negotiate a new loan to absorb the national debt at a lower rate of interest. The funding bill passed over Morrill's objection.[58]

In 1869 Morrill again urged Congress to support refinancing the national debt at a lower interest rate and elevating the treasury notes to par with gold coins. He dismissed as "dubious" the argument that any renegotiation of the national debt should wait because "terms sufficiently advantageous would not be proposed and accepted." Funding the debt at the "lowest practicable rate" was of "primary importance." Morrill also suggested redeeming legal-tender notes with federal interest-bearing bonds. "It is undoubtedly the cheapest mode of getting these notes redeemed and out of the road to an ultimate resumption of specie payments."[59] This argument succeeded. The resultant bill, signed by

President Grant on 18 March 1869, pledged the federal government to pay all obligations in coin or its equivalent, except when the original agreement made other provisions.[60]

The 1869 bill strengthened the public credit, so Treasury Secretary Boutwell presented Congress a detailed plan for refunding the debt in his December 1869 report. The Finance Committee responded with a bill limiting the length of bonds' redeemability to no more than twenty years. The House insisted on thirty years for 4 percent bonds to make them more attractive to investors. The Refunding Acts of 14 July 1870, and 20 January 1871, authorized the Treasury to issue $500 million bonds at 5 percent redeemable in ten years, $300 million at 4.5 percent redeemable in fifteen years, and $1 billion at 4 percent redeemable after thirty years. The Treasury would redeem all bonds with coin. All were exempt from taxes, and none could be sold at less than par with gold.[61]

Morrill continued urging the resumption of specie payment for United States notes, even after the Panic of 1873. He believed conditions were right: the notes had risen nearly to par with gold; exchange rates had gold flowing into the country; there was a ready market for exports; and debts had been reduced to a minimum. To him, "adherence to paper money alone is adherence to panics." Not to act when conditions were favorable "would be an inexcusable neglect of duty on the part of legislators." The pressure from greenback supporters was too great, however, and Congress failed to pass Morrill's resumption bill.[62]

A determined Morrill introduced another specie resumption bill in January 1875. (Every year since 1866, he had urged Congress to resume specie payments.) Legal-tender notes were a temporary war measure, he explained, and "not to be indefinitely protracted in time of peace." In a classic understatement, he continued, "It is hardly necessary for me to say that I am not an ardent lover of incontrovertible paper money, but an inflexible supporter of a speedy return to specie payments, sincerely believing the dearest interests of our country imperatively require it."[63] This time Morrill succeeded. The law, as President Grant signed it, created a system of free banking, retired greenbacks up to 80 percent of new national bank notes issued until the level decreased to $300 million (which would continue to circulate indefinitely), withdrew paper fractional currency and replaced it with silver coins, removed the coinage charge for gold, and resumed specie payments on 1 January 1879.[64]

When Pres. Rutherford B. Hayes assumed office in March 1877, John Sherman became treasury secretary. With Sherman's appointment,

Morrill became Finance Committee chair. Morrill apparently could have had a cabinet position, but preferred to remain in the Senate. With James Garfield's election in 1882, Sherman was no longer treasury secretary. After his reelection to the Senate, he expected to resume his former position as Finance Committee chair. Most committee members, however, preferred Morrill's leadership, so he declined to step aside. Sherman was disappointed. Although he and Morrill continued to have high regard for each other, they were never as close as before.[65]

Morrill used the Finance Committee chair as a "bully pulpit" for sound money. With the greenback question settled, at least temporarily, silver became the vehicle to inflate the economy and, therefore, sound money's newest nemesis. In July 1876 Missouri congressman Richard P. Bland introduced a bill providing free and unlimited coinage of silver. After the bill passed the House, Iowa senator William B. Allison amended it to restore silver to legal tender and to authorize the treasury secretary to purchase not less than $2 million or more than $4 million in silver bullion each month and mint it into coin. Morrill wrote Interior Secretary Carl Schurz suggesting he join with Treasury Secretary Sherman to "keep the administration right" in opposing "remonetizing" the silver dollar. He continued that if the federal government set a silver-to-gold ratio of 16:1, it would be "fatal to the future greatness of our country—worse if possible than paper legal tender."[66] Schurz assured Morrill that President Hayes was "too cautious a man" to directly oppose his treasury secretary. He then suggested that Morrill return to Washington early because, "There may be an opportunity, if not necessity, for consultation."[67]

Farmers, westerners, debtors, and silver miners pressured their representatives to pass the Bland-Allison bill; so despite the opposition of Morrill and the administration, the bill passed both houses of Congress. Hayes vetoed the bill, but Congress overrode the veto in 1878. The reaction against the administration's opposition to the bill helped carry the Democrats to victory in 1878 and gave them control over both the House and the Senate. This cost Morrill his chair, beginning with the 1879 term. He would regain it in 1883 and hold it until his death, except for the 1893–95 term when Democrats again controlled the Senate. But even when the Republicans were out of power, Democrats sought his advice and counsel. Morrill supported Pres. Grover Cleveland's sound money policies, but opposed him on the tariff.[68]

During the twelve years the Bland-Allison Act remained in effect, the Treasury coined $378 million in silver dollars. Neither banks nor the public liked the heavy coins. The government promoted public usage, but Treasury Secretary Sherman admitted in 1880 that he could not keep 35 percent of the coined silver dollars in circulation. Morrill noted in 1883 that the Treasury held nearly $94 million in silver coins and another $141 million in silver bullion "that the Government would be only too glad to unload."[69]

In 1890 Congress passed and Pres. Benjamin Harrison signed the Silver Act authorizing the treasury secretary to purchase 4.5 million ounces of silver bullion each month and to pay for it with legal tender treasury notes. After 1 July 1891, the mint would coin only enough silver dollars to redeem notes. When Grover Cleveland regained the presidency in 1893, he demanded relief from the silver purchases. Gold reserves were down to $96 million. In June 1893, Great Britain closed Indian mints to the free coinage of silver. A financial panic followed. Cleveland called Congress into special session in August and by 30 October 1893, both houses had repealed the Treasury's requirement to purchase silver. The 1896 presidential election between William Jennings Bryan and William McKinley centered on the money issue. Calling Bryan's prosilver platform a "debt-paying scheme of repudiation," Morrill actively supported McKinley. In November 1896, the voters favored McKinley and gold over Bryan and silver. McKinley's victory laid the silver issue to rest, temporarily.[70]

Although Morrill was the author of important legislation in the Senate, none compared to the Land Grant College Act or Civil War tariff bills. His position as Finance Committee chair made him one of the most powerful people in Washington. He also served on several other committees, including Buildings and Grounds. After Morrill's election to the Senate, Washington became his second home. As Buildings and Grounds chair, he had a lasting impact on the beauty and grandeur of the city and Capitol.

Notes

1. Morrill, speech, "An Exclusively Paper Currency Inconsistent with Permanent Prosperity," delivered in the House of Representatives, 24 January 1867, LOC.
2. Parker, *Morrill*, 185; E. L. Woodbridge to Morrill, 22 April 1867; John Wilder to John Gardner, 14 May 1867, LOC.
3. Parker, *Morrill*, 185–86.
4. Ibid., 186–87.
5. Ibid.

6. Ibid., 188–89.
7. Ibid.
8. Ibid., 189–91.
9. Ibid., 190–91.
10. Ibid., 203.
11. Ibid., 193–94.
12. Ibid., 195.
13. Ibid., 196–98.
14. Morrill to Ruth, 28 June 1867, LOC.
15. Parker, *Morrill*, 203.
16. Ibid., 206.
17. Ibid., 203.
18. Ibid., 184, 204–6.
19. Morrill to Ruth, 28 June 1867, LOC.
20. See above 107-8.
21. Kenneth M. Stampp, *The Era of Reconstruction: 1865–1877* (New York: Vintage Books, 1967), 111–12.
22. See above 107-8.
23. Stampp, *Era of Reconstruction,* 112–14.
24. Ibid., 113–18.
25. Ibid., 146–47. When the session ended on 3 March 1867, the Fortieth Congress convened the following day.
26. Ibid.
27. Ibid., 148–49; Foner, *Reconstruction,* 333.
28. Stampp, *Era of Reconstruction,* 148–50; Foner, *Reconstruction,* 334–35.
29. John Bingham (Ohio), George Boutwell and Benjamin Butler (Massachusetts), John Logan (Illinois), Thaddeus Stevens and Thomas Williams (Pennsylvania) and James Wilson (Iowa).
30. Stampp, *Era of Reconstruction,* 150–51; Foner, *Reconstruction,* 334–35.
31. Foner, *Reconstruction,* 335–36.
32. Some historians, including David Donald in *The Politics of Reconstruction: 1863–67* (Cambridge: Harvard University Press, 1984), considered Morrill a Radical. Although he often voted with the Radicals, Morrill supported positions that were good for Vermont and good for the country. He was a loyal Republican, but he was not afraid to take an independent stance.
33. Undated notes in Morrill's handwriting; Morrill to Ruth, 28 June 1867, LOC.
34. Morrill to Fessenden, 10 May 1868, quoted in Parker, *Morrill*, 211.
35. Ibid.
36. Parker, *Morrill*, 212–15.
37. Morrill to Charles Sumner, quoted in Parker, *Morrill*, 231.
38. Parker, *Morrill*, 212–15.
39. Foner, *Reconstruction,* 336; Parker, *Morrill*, 214; Fessenden, *William Pitt Fessenden*, 2:207.
40. Parker, *Morrill*, 321.
41. Morrill to Whitlaw Reid, 15 May 1884, quoted in Parker, *Morrill*, 303.
42. Parker, *Morrill*, 247.

43. Ibid., 229, 244–47.
44. Morrill to Secretary of State Hamilton Fish, 18 July 1870; Morrill to Charles Sumner, 10 September 1870; Morrill to Sumner, September 1870, LOC.
45. Morrill to Greeley, 11 March 1872, LOC.
46. Ibid.; Greeley to Morrill, 12 March 1872, LOC.
47. Morrill to John A. Page, 11 April 1873, LOC.
48. Morrill to G. G. Benedict, printed in the *Burlington Free Press and Times,* 27 June 1873, LOC.
49. Parker, *Morrill,* 227.
50. Ibid., 182.
51. See chapter three on the Morrill Tariff.
52. Dewey, *Financial History,* 142–43; Sharkey, *Money, Class, and Party,* 339–42.
53. Sharkey, *Money, Class, and Party,* 66–67.
54. Dewey, *Financial History,* 335–37; Sharkey, *Money, Class, and Party,* 71–72.
55. Sharkey, *Money, Class, and Party,* 73–80; Dewey, *Financial History,* 340–42.
56. Sharkey, *Money, Class, and Party,* 83–84; Dewey, *Financial History,* 341–343; Morrill, speech, "A bill to raise the value of legal-tender notes to par," delivered in the Senate, 11 December 1867, LOC.
57. Morrill, speech, "The Funding Bill," delivered in the Senate, 3 March 1868, LOC.
58. Ibid.
59. Morrill, speech, "Public Debt and Funding," delivered in the Senate, 11 February 1869, LOC.
60. Dewey, *Financial History,* 349.
61. Sharkey, *Money, Class, and Party,* 130; Dewey, *Financial History,* 352–53.
62. Morrill, speech, "Free Banking and Specie Payments," delivered in the Senate, 4 December 1873, LOC.
63. Morrill, speech, "Resumption of Specie Payments," delivered in the Senate, 5 January 1875; Morrill to G. G. Benedict, 22 October 1875, LOC.
64. Dewey, *Financial History,* 372–73.
65. Parker, *Morrill,* 300–301.
66. Morrill to Schurz, 4 June 1877, LOC.
67. Schurz to Morrill, 5 June 1877, LOC.
68. Dewey, *Financial History,* 406–8.
69. Parker, *Morrill,* 172; Morrill, speech, "Coinage, Silver Certificates, and United States Notes," delivered in the Senate, 5 December 1883, LOC.
70. Dewey, *Financial History,* 436–62; Morrill, speech, "Free Coinage of Silver," no date or place given; Morrill, speech, "Free Coinage Substitute for the House Bond Bill," delivered in the Senate 1 February 1896, Morrill to A. E. Parker, 30 June 1896; Morrill to F. T. Williams, 20 July 1896; Morrill to George Shoop, 3 August 1896; Morrill to W. F. Stipe, 12 August 1896, LOC.

8

Beautifying Washington

The Capitol is a credit to the nation. The architectural proportions are superb. The interior is arranged very ingeniously and with great solidity. The sculpture, the paintings and costly trappings are worth a look. . . . The grounds, nature and art, have nearly made perfect.[1]

Justin Morrill, 1841

Justin Morrill loved Washington. After his election to the Senate, he decided to build a second home there. This made his life more comfortable and allowed him to fulfill his social obligations as a leading senator. Then, as Buildings and Grounds Committee chair, he had the opportunity to make the city even more beautiful and worthy of being the capital of a great nation.

In his first years in the House of Representatives, Morrill lived in a boardinghouse while Congress was in session. Later, he rented a house and brought his family to be with him for the winter session. Now the Morrills would have their own home in Washington. Morrill chose a corner lot at number one Thomas Circle, near the city's edge, but in a "well-established, solidly genteel neighborhood."[2] When told he could get a much larger lot farther out on Rhode Island Avenue, he replied that he did not feel "the blood of the pioneer sufficiently strong in my veins to push out into the wilderness."[3]

The senator hired Edward Clark, the Capitol architect, to design the house. Completed in 1871, it was not lavish, but it was roomy and comfortable. Two-storied with a mansard roof that essentially added a third floor, it had several fireplaces like those Clark had included in the Capitol offices. The bathrooms had gilded fixtures, specially ordered from New York. The sitting room featured four oval paintings in the ceiling by Constantino Brumidi, whose work also adorned the Capitol. Italian artwork, gathered for Morrill by his friend Minister to Rome George Perkins Marsh and by Morrill himself during his European tour, decorated the walls. Sculptor Larkin Mead, who lived in Venice, also acquired paintings and other works of art for Morrill. French porcelain, clocks, and vases added an elegant touch. As with his Strafford home, Morrill's favorite room must have been the library. Here, before the open fire, he could discuss state and national politics with Republican Party leaders or spend a quiet evening with his books.[4]

In 1885, however, Dr. W. W. Johnston's plans for the adjacent property threatened the serenity of Morrill's library. Morrill was disturbed to learn that a change in Dr. Johnston's blueprints would place the kitchen very close to Morrill's library window. Morrill complained to Johnston's architects that the change would expose his library to "the constant affliction" of the "perpetual smells of the kitchen." His only "escape" would be to erect "a solid wall . . . to shut off the prospective nuisance." He also believed Johnston's house would be so near the street it would detract from Morrill's home. Dr. Johnston wanted to reach some agreement with Morrill. Morrill responded he would do nothing "in the way of retaliation or ill temper, but it may be necessary for me to do something to prevent my estate from diminishing in value."[5] They must have found some compromise, for Johnston built his house and there is no indication that Morrill sued.

The Washington home allowed the Morrills to display their Vermont hospitality. Friends and relatives from Vermont often stayed with them while visiting the nation's capital. Old friends and neighbors, including Gen. William T. Sherman, North Carolina senator Zebulon B. Vance, Ohio senator Henry B. Payne, and Rhode Island senator Henry B. Anthony, gathered at the Morrill home for whist nearly every evening. President Grant dined there on the eve of his retirement. Beginning in 1880, Senator Morrill's annual birthday party became one of Washington's social events of the year. The Burlington *Free Press* described one celebration attended by "President McKinley, Secretary Porter, Vice President Hobart . . . and almost the entire congressional contingent, with other distinguished members of the local society." The "elegant home . . . was beautifully decorated with choice roses and palms." Guests enjoyed a buffet supper "served during the evening in the dining room from a table decorated in pink." As usual Ruth and Louise graciously presided over the affair.[6]

When Morrill moved into his Washington home, he purchased a matching pair of black horses and a $910 Rockaway carriage. Every morning this beautiful equipage carried him to the Senate, "where he had no rival in punctuality or length of attendance."[7] Later, he found he could hire a driver and two-horse carriage cheaper than keeping his own. After 1882, he continued to arrive promptly, but in a rented carriage.[8]

These were years of political power and prestige for Justin Morrill. His Senate seat was secure. As Finance Committee chair, he held one of the most powerful positions in the federal government. Administrative, judicial, and congressional members of both political parties held him in high esteem. Nearly forty years earlier, when he had visited Washington, Morrill indicated he had no desire to serve "without eminence." Perhaps this desire helped impel him to become one of the most eminent public servants of his day.

The slower pace in the Senate also provided Morrill time for other, more leisurely activities. Between 1879 and 1881, when Democrats controlled the Senate and he did not have the time-consuming position as Finance Committee chair, Morrill compiled his notes based on his years of reading into a small book for his friends. *Self-Consciousness of Noted Persons*, with 81 pages and 116 "noted persons" in the first edition and 187 pages and 171 persons in the second, cited "extracts from various authors, showing both well-founded and ill-founded ambition to be held in remembrance by posterity."[9] The book encompassed men from the ancient times to the contemporary, including Demosthenes, Saint Paul, Montaigne, Sir Walter Scott, Ethan Allen, and abolitionist Owen Lovejoy.

Morrill also found time to serve on the Smithsonian Board of Regents beginning in 1883. In 1894 he introduced a bill to amend the act that established the institution in 1845. The amendment allowed the Smithsonian to accept gifts or bequests of money and property. In a speech supporting the bill, Morrill explained the museum had been so successful in gathering important materials and artifacts and "diffusing practical knowledge" that it had outgrown its facility. The change in the law would allow the organization to construct an additional building, just west of the original. The Smithsonian could then preserve and exhibit "a very large amount of accumulated material now unhappily stored away" and would have space for future growth.[10]

Also during this more leisurely time in 1880, Morrill and his family retraced his earlier European tour. Secretary of State William M. Evarts smoothed the path by instructing all American consulars and diplomats to treat the senator as an officer of the United States and to grant him all the "courteous attentions" within their power. Justin, Ruth, Louise, and James sailed on the *Celtic* on 3 July. Since Morrill had his family with him on this trip, he wrote little of his journey and so we know few details of their travels. They visited England, France, Switzerland, and Italy. Rome with its Coliseum and other magnificent historic structures, which he had skipped before, greatly impressed Morrill. While in Italy, he visited his friend Larkin Mead again. Mead would later create bas-relief panels for the Washington Monument. The entire family enjoyed their trip, James especially so.[11]

James had moved with the family into their Washington home. Then in 1876 he attended Dartmouth College in Hanover, New Hampshire, near Strafford. James would follow his mother's family into medicine. He changed his mind in 1879 and left Dartmouth without graduating. He then enrolled in the University of Vermont and became an attorney. Although he apparently practiced law for a while, James spent much of his time tending his father's business affairs.[12]

In 1887 James was stricken with typhoid fever while checking on Justin's investment in the Brierfield, Alabama, coalfields. He attempted to return to Strafford, but only managed to reach Washington. The senator, at Amherst College to deliver a speech, immediately left for Washington. Ruth and Louise caught the first available train to join them. The train, however, crashed at Havre de Grace, Maryland. The women escaped through a window. Ruth was uninjured, but Louise suffered severe bruises. Although James's crisis passed after nine weeks, symptoms still lingered years later. His illness may have been the reason James later became Justin's private secretary instead of pursuing his own career in law.[13]

With their new home in Washington, the Morrills spent summers at Strafford and winters in the capital. Post-Civil War Washington was very different from the city Morrill had visited in 1841. The population had grown to 126,000 in 1867, nearly double that of the prewar years. The war had left Washington a shabby place. Troops had stripped the city of trees for firewood. Piles of rotting mule carcasses lay behind makeshift stables along the Capitol Mall. New York *Tribune* editor Horace Greeley described the post-war capital as a place "where the rents are high, the food is bad, the dust is disgusting, the mud is deep, and the morals are deplorable."[14] Greeley urged Congress to move the capital to St. Louis.

To counteract such a move, Washington businessmen petitioned Congress in 1870 to create the Territory of the District of Columbia. Congress complied with the request. President Grant appointed banker Jay Cooke's brother Henry as territorial governor and named another crony, Alexander Shepherd, to the Board of Public Works. Shepherd ordered a massive rebuilding project, including demolishing old buildings, removing railroad tracks, paving streets, placing sewers underground, filling canals, and planting 60,000 trees. Within two years Shepherd spent more than $2 million and obligated the territory for another $9.4 million. By the summer of 1873, the District was bankrupt. This led to the failure of Jay Cooke's bank and contributed to the Panic of 1873. Henry Cooke resigned and Grant appointed Shepherd as governor. Public outcry led to a congressional investigation. Investigators concluded the Washington territorial experiment had proven to be a costly and corrupt failure and Congress dissolved the territorial government. Shepherd, meanwhile, fled to Chihuahua, Mexico.[15]

Despite the corruption and gross mismanagement, Shepherd created a "new Washington." New York *Independent* correspondent Mary Clemmer Ames described 1873 Washington as a cosmopolitan city with "broad carriage drives, level as floors . . . plat on plat of restful grass parks, [with] double rows of young trees . . . as far as sight could reach. . . . Peace, prosperity and luxury have taken the place of war, of knightly days and of heroic men."[16]

Justin Morrill also want the nation to have a capital it could be proud of. He told fellow senators, "Washington is no mean city. It is the capital of the people; and its public buildings and grounds belong to the Nation, and they will be jealously guarded as the apple of its eye."[17] Even while still in the House, he had pushed a bill through Congress to convert the Old Hall of the House of Representatives into a national Statuary Hall where each state placed two statues of its "typical" men. Vermont selected Ethan Allen and Sen. Jacob Collamer. Morrill apparently first met Larkin Mead when he received the commission to sculpt the Ethan Allen bust. Hiriam Powers, whose studio Morrill had visited in Venice in 1867, did the Collamer bust.[18]

Determined to keep railroad tracks from marring the Capitol's setting, Morrill opposed the Pennsylvania Railroad's extension into the Capitol

Mall in 1872. His reaction was in such strong language that the Senate considered it too severe for parliamentary usage and ordered it stricken from the record. Members and observers must have been surprised at such an outburst from the dignified senator from Vermont. Constituents recalled Morrill had mockingly suggested inviting the railroad's vice president to the Senate floor to dictate legislation affecting the company. He explained he did not want to prevent railroads in Washington, but he wanted them in the "right place." Despite his opposition, Congress approved the extension. Thirty-five years later, the federal government vindicated Morrill's position by paying the Pennsylvania Railroad $1.5 million to remove its tracks from the Mall.[19]

Spending more time in Washington allowed Morrill to watch over the many projects his Committee on Buildings and Grounds generated. He told his colleagues, "I confess to a feeling of some reverence for this Capitol, where I have spent so many years of my life."[20] In June 1874 the committee hired Frederick Law Olmstead to completely redesign the Capitol grounds. The renovation included a 100-foot wide carriage court running the entire length of the Capitol's east side. For ease of entry, the court would be near street level and have seven entrances. Olmstead proposed removing the trees remaining on the east side and excavating six feet of dirt to lower the grounds to the desired level. The result would be a park-like setting with a nearly flat surface and long curving paths and roads. Trees, in "natural groupings" would give added beauty.[21]

Olmstead suggested widening the 30-foot terrace on the Capitol's west side to fifty feet. He would replace the building's facade with a "wall of marble corresponding in dimensions and architectural character to those of the wings." "Grand staircases" would lead from the terrace to the ground below. A wide walkway would connect the staircases with other walks entering the building. The effect of these changes would be to "greatly increase the apparent height and massiveness of that part of the building supporting the dome." Olmstead estimated the first year's work would cost between $200,000 and 300,000. Morrill proposed also adding statues of Layfayette and Columbus near the western approach to the Capitol.[22]

Work began immediately. Olmstead catalogued all the trees on the Capitol's east side: at least 400 were diseased or "dilapidated," and he would have to remove them; others he saved for replanting. Olmstead's plan to destroy several old elm trees on the Capitol's south side met with opposition from Sen. Simon Cameron, also a member of the Buildings and Grounds Committee. Olmstead explained to Morrill that the tree

Cameron wanted to preserve interfered with a planned walkway. Workers would have to excavate several feet of dirt to keep within the approved plan. Since adjoining curbs and roadways were already complete, changing the plan to accommodate the tree would involve much work and extra cost. Olmstead hoped Morrill would "induce" Cameron to withdraw his objections.[23]

Cameron also wrote Morrill. While appreciating the changes to the Capitol grounds, Cameron did not want to destroy "that beautiful tree that I have admired for more than 30 years." Olmstead had told Cameron the tree was dying. But after a careful inspection, Cameron concluded, "if left alone it will be erect and beautiful long, long, after I leave here." He ended his letter with the plea, "Woodman spare that tree." Morrill agreed and the tree was "spared."[24]

Since Olmstead divided his time between New York and Washington during the project, Capitol Architect Edward Clark oversaw the work during Olmstead's absence. In July 1874 Clark estimated that 1,000 men were working on the east side grounds. By August workers had removed the designated trees and excavated 15,000 yards of dirt. The work progressed well, despite a couple of minor problems. During a period when Olmstead was in New York and Clark was on vacation, contractors delivered thousands of loads of soil and manure on the wrong side of the building. Laborers had to move it all by hand. Work also stopped for a day when an "International" incited a mob into demanding wages 50 percent above the standard rate. The next day police on the scene prevented further demonstrations.[25]

Congress appropriated money for the Capitol improvements in stages. For example, the grounds were finished in 1876 but the west terrace was not completed until 1886. The changes enhanced the beauty of both the Capitol and its setting. As work on the Capitol progressed, Congress considered the Washington Monument. Construction had begun in 1848, but stopped around 1850. The half-finished structure had set as a giant eyesore ever since. In 1876 Congress appropriated money to finish the job. Although Morrill apparently wanted the "chimney," as it was scornfully known, torn down and redesigned, he reluctantly supported finishing the project using the original design. As the monument neared completion, Morrill helped Mead secure the commission for four bas-reliefs to adorn the monument.[26]

Later the senator served on the dedication committee. Morrill tried to persuade Oliver Wendell Holmes to read a poem at the celebration on

Washington's Birthday in 1885, but Holmes declined saying he felt unequal to the effort. Robert C. Winthrop, who delivered the address at the laying of the cornerstone in 1848, was to speak at the dedication. Poor health prevented him from attending, but his friend John D. Long read Winthrop's prepared remarks.[27]

Although Morrill was intimately involved with the Capitol grounds' beautification and the Washington Monument's completion, a new building for the Library of Congress was the project closest to his heart. Founded in 1800, the Library occupied space inside the Capitol. When the British burned the building in 1814, the Library burned, too. By the 1860s the collection had outgrown its space. In 1872 Congress authorized $5,000 prizes for plans for a new building, even though many members preferred to modify the Capitol to make room. Morrill, a lover of books and learning, strongly supported the Library, but adamantly opposed any effort to add an extension onto the Capitol.[28]

In an 1879 speech to the Senate, Morrill explained the need for more space and his opposition to a Capitol annex as home to the Library. The present facility could not hold the books already in it. More than 70,000 volumes, which was larger than the entire collection in 1860, were "tumbled about on the floor or stacked up in alcoves wholly inaccessible." Such conditions spoke "volumes for more room." In addition, the Library was adding between 30,000 and 40,000 books each year. Morrill told the senators, "The unyielding truth is that we have to move Congress out to give room for the Library, or move the Library out to give room for Congress."[29]

He believed an annex would provide inadequate space and detract from the Capitol itself. "Any extension, which could possibly furnish one-fourth part of the room needed for a new Library of Congress would not only cruelly distort the Capitol itself, utterly destroying its admirable singleness of design, but would be an equally flagrant maltreatment of the Capitol grounds." Morrill then compared the Capitol's setting to Versailles.[30] He obviously felt protective of the work Olmstead was doing.

Morrill shared his vision of "courts, libraries, museums, and departmental offices" around the grounds on the Capitol's east side. He admitted the idea was "progressive and possibly too magnificent." But, he elaborated, if the "executive department" had originally been "constructed around one large square," the arrangement would have been much more convenient and presented a more "imposing" appearance. "I have advocated the erection of a separate Library building on a part of these grounds east of the Capitol, because it would be most convenient and cost the least money, and because a separate building seems to me to be a pressing necessity."[31]

The rest of Congress could not see the "pressing necessity" of a separate Library building and refused to commit funds. Morrill tried again the following year in 1880. He spoke against the "Reconstruction of the Capitol" and for Indiana senator Daniel W. Voorhees's bill to establish a committee to select a permanent site for the Library. "I am for the Library out and out," he said, "and as much against remodeling and rebuilding the Capitol."[32] Evoking a bit of humor, he informed his colleagues, "The battle of the books, nearly one hundred thousand strong . . . has been raging on the floor of the Library for some years." Within ten years the Library would need at least "two and a half acres" to house its collection.[33]

Morrill ridiculed the proposal to create extra space by remodeling the Capitol. He expressed his reverence for the building and its site. The people, he believed, were proud of the Capitol and did not want it "hacked to pieces to give temporary accommodation to the Library," especially when a separate building would cost less money. Instead, he offered an amendment to create a commission to select the best site for a new Library building.[34]

In 1881 the Senate considered a bill to construct a separate Library building. Morrill again suggested the site just east of the Capitol (where the Library of Congress now stands). He denied being dogmatic or rigid, but that site was superior to any other. It was "near at hand, elevated, dry, and healthy, with all the adhering advantages of its surroundings." In addition to the natural beauty of this site, its proximity to the Capitol made it more accessible and convenient than any other. Still Congress did not act.[35]

Morrill tried again in 1886. He proposed allotting $550,000 to purchase the site he had long advocated. The price was below market value and would include the removal of structures already on the property. Morrill admitted that some people suggested locating the Library of Congress on property already owned by the government. But after considering that possibility for years, he concluded, "there are no vacant grounds belonging now to the Government which even the pages of the Senate would recommend for a library site." An architect estimated that a Library capable of holding more than three million books would cost

$3,262,600, in addition to the land. He "urgently" asked the senators to "appreciate the importance of taking care of the most valuable library now existing on the American continent."[36]

At last the Senate agreed and approved the measure to buy the land by a forty-five to eight vote. The House quickly concurred. After fourteen years, Morrill had succeeded. A reporter described the stately senator from Vermont as forgetting his dignity, "his most conspicuous characteristic," and throwing Senator Voorhees a kiss. Voorhees responded with a similar gesture. A page brought congressional librarian Spofford to the Senate chamber. An observer noted that Morrill, Voorhees, and Spofford "embraced each other warmly," and then after handshakes and congratulations "the little love feast ended."[37]

An example of the esteem with which Morrill's colleagues held him occurred later in the 1886 session, after the Senate had finally approved the Library of Congress Building. Morrill became too ill to attend Senate proceedings. During his absence, the Senate voted to omit $50,000 for a federal building in Montpelier from a funding bill. Not wanting to disappoint Morrill, Wisconsin senator John Spooner suggested amending the bill to include the money. Spooner explained, "The Senator from Vermont was anxious about this, and . . . it would be a graceful and handsome compliment to that Senator, who for the first time in twenty years of service here, is absent from the Senate during its session."[38] After calling Morrill the "Father of the Senate," Spooner suggested the Senate amend the bill by "unanimous consent." His colleagues concurred and reinstated $50,000 for Montpelier's federal building.

Two years after approving money to buy the building site Congress authorized $6 million to build the Library. The final cost was $6,003,140, or $.595 per square foot. Morrill must have felt a sense of pride when the beautiful building opened in 1897. No one had worked harder or more persistently for the Library of Congress than he.[39]

With funding for the Library secured, Morrill addressed another need on 13 December 1898: a separate building for the Supreme Court, which was also housed in the Capitol. A recent gas explosion and fire that damaged the court's quarters "sternly indicate[d]" the need for "a more appropriate home" for "that rather neglected coordinate branch" of government. The site Morrill suggested was near the Library of Congress on the Capitol's east side. "The ground is so obviously indispensable to complete the symmetry of the grounds on the eastern front of the Capitol," he argued, "no Senator would deny that its ultimate acquisition is . . . as fixed as Milton's 'fate, free-will, and foreknowledge absolute.'" It was indeed fortunate such a necessary piece of land could also serve as site for the Supreme Court.[40]

Morrill praised his predecessors for their foresight in selecting the Capitol location. He noted, however, that they had underestimated the country's growth rate and had approved buildings too small to serve the public need. As the United States grew from thirteen to forty-five states, the demand for Senate and House office space quickly outstripped the supply. The legislature needed every square foot of room in the Capitol. So it made sense to build a separate structure, suitable for the Supreme Court, on adjacent land. "The elevation upon which the Capitol stands . . . adds immensely to its dignity, and with the Library and Supreme Court buildings situated not far apart thereon, they will form a harmonious group of large public structures on Capitol Hill of unequaled grandeur, and will be appreciated by the American people forever."[41] The Senate approved the measure that same day, and Morrill encouraged the House to follow suit. Unfortunately, however, he would not be available to guide the project to its conclusion. This was his last speech. Two weeks later, on 28 December 1898, Morrill died from pneumonia.[42]

Washington and the Capitol captivated Morrill when he first visited in 1841. This affection and admiration continued for the rest of his life. After becoming Senate Buildings and Grounds Committee chair, he was the city's strongest advocate in Congress. To him belonged much credit for preserving the beauty of the Capitol's setting and the building's integrity. His vision also made the Library of Congress building a reality. City residents passed a resolution thanking him for his "manly efforts." Senator Simon Cameron also acknowledged Morrill's role: "You will have the honor, after you are dead, of having made the most beautiful city in the world and what is more you will deserve it."[43]

Chapter 8

1. Morrill, "Wanderings and Scribblings; or Journal of a Journey South and West in May, June, and July, 1841," LOC.
2. Kathryn Allamong Jacob, *Capital Elites: High Society in Washington, D.C., after the Civil War* (Washington: Smithsonian Institution Press, 1995), 79.
3. Parker, *Morrill*, 222.
4. Ibid., 222–225; M. Gibbs to Morrill, 5 May and 22 November 1871; Archer and Pancoast to Morrill, 18 November 1871, LOC; interview with Gwenda Smith.

5. Morrill to Hornblower and Marshall, 28 July and 2 August 1885; Morrill to Johnston, 27 August 1885, LOC.

6. *Burlington Free Press and Times,* April 1897, LOC; Parker, *Morrill,* 222–26.

7. Parker, *Morrill,* 227.

8. Morrill to H. E. Hall and Snow, 30 September 1871; Kimball Brothers to Morrill, 28 November 1871; Morrill to Ruth, 23 July 1882, LOC.

9. Parker, *Morrill,* 324–25.

10. Senate bill, untitled, 18 January 1894; Morrill, speech, ca. January 1894, LOC.

11. Parker, *Morrill,* 297–98; Evarts to Diplomats and Consular Officers of the United States in Europe, 4 June 1880; Mead to Morrill, 30 September 1880, LOC.

12. Morrill to James Morrill, 1876; T. J. Peter to Morrill, 5 May 1886, LOC; *New York Times,* "Mrs. Morrill," 5 February 1896; *Burlington Free Press and Times,* 3 October 1898; interview with Gwenda Smith.

13. "James Morrill's Illness," *Boston Journal,* 23 June 1887; Stanley Matthews to Morrill, 26 June 1887; T. J. Peter to Morrill, 5 May 1886; Morrill to James G. Blaine, 18 December 1887; Susan Edmunds to Morrill, 9 September 1890, LOC.

14. Jacob, *Capital Elites,* 55.

15. Ibid., 55–56.

16. Ibid., 57.

17. Parker, *Morrill,* 250.

18. Ibid., 247–48.

19. Ibid., 249; Morrill to D. D. Foley, 15 June 1874, LOC.

20. Parker, *Morrill,* 250.

21. Olmstead to Morrill, 9 June 1874, LOC.

22. Ibid.; Olmstead to Morrill, 22 May 1874; Morrill, Senate Resolution, 6 January 1886, LOC.

23. Olmstead to Morrill, 14 September 1875, LOC.

24. Cameron to Morrill, 27 September 1875, LOC; Parker, *Morrill,* 251.

25. Olmstead to Morrill, 20 July and 16 August 1874; Clark to Morrill, 22 August 1874, LOC.

26. Parker, *Morrill,* 249–52, 310–11; Mead to Morrill, 29 November 1880, and 29 March 1881, LOC.

27. George W. Weaver to Morrill, 21 May 1884; Morrill to Winthrop, 3 June, 13 September, and 25 September 1884; Morrill to Holmes, 13 September 1884; Amos Lawrence to Morrill, 8 January 1885; Winthrop to Morrill, 13 February 1885; Morrill to Winthrop, 23 February 1885, LOC.

28. Parker, *Morrill,* 252–53; Morrill, speech, "The Library of Congress," delivered in the Senate, 31 March 1879, LOC.

29. Morrill, speech, "Library of Congress."

30. Ibid.

31. Ibid.

32. Morrill, speech, "Against the Reconstruction of the Capitol, and in Favor of a Commission to Select a Site for a New Library," delivered in the Senate, 13 May 1880, LOC.

33. Ibid.

34. Ibid.

35. Morrill, speech, "Congressional Library," delivered in the Senate, 21 February 1881, LOC.
36. Morrill, "Remarks," ca. January 1886, LOC.
37. Parker, *Morrill*, 322.
38. Ibid.
39. Ibid., 252–53, 321–22; D. W. Voorhees to Morrill, 2 August 1886; Morrill to Voorhees, 24 August 1894; Casey [Capitol architect] to Morrill, 24 December 1894, LOC.
40. Morrill, speech, "Upon a Proposed Site for the Supreme Court of the United States," delivered in the Senate, 13 December 1898, LOC.
41. Ibid.
42. Morrill to Melville Fuller, 17 December 1898, Chicago Historical Society.
43. Cameron to Morrill, 24 October 1874; Resolution of Appreciation from Washington Citizens Association, 3 July 1888, LOC.

EPILOGUE

He was absolutely incorruptible. I do not speak of corruption by money, which is only the vice of vulgar souls. But he was not to be swerved by ambition, by party influence, by desire to please friends or by fear of displeasing enemies, or by currents of popular passion. Oh, the loss of him, the loss of him, in this awful crisis that is upon us now! His death is a substantial diminution of the security of the republic.[1]

Senator George L. Hoar

Justin Morrill's death came suddenly, but it must not have been too surprising to his friends and family. He was eighty-eight years old and physical strength had begun to wane. The previous year he suffered a severe cold and bronchitis, but recovered. His health had never been hardy and throughout his years in Congress he experienced bouts of "grip" (influenza) and other illnesses. He carefully guarded his health and once even declined to serve as House Ways and Means chair because he considered the duties too taxing on his system. Still, even at eighty-eight, he maintained a full schedule, serving on several Senate committees in addition to Finance and Buildings and Grounds.

Although his colleagues greatly respected the Senate's senior member, Morrill did not wield the political influence he once did. In 1897 his longtime friend and supporter G. G. Benedict applied for the collectorship for the port of Burlington. Morrill backed Benedict's candidacy. The Vermont delegation, led by Sen. Redfield Proctor, ignored Morrill's plea and selected Olin Merrill for the position. Morrill wrote his friend

Benedict, "It was the first time in my life that I felt the shame of deserting a friend." He then explained he had only given up the fight when he "thought the contest could no longer be maintained with credit to you, myself or the state."[2] Benedict thanked Morrill for his support, saying he did not feel Morrill "deserted" him, "You did all that you could for any man."[3] Still, it must have wounded Morrill to realize he could not sway his own state's delegation to appoint an old friend.

He suffered his most severe blow, however, on 13 May 1898, when his beloved Ruth died. Louise recalled that a few days before his death she had noticed a pained look on his face. When asked if he were ill, Justin replied, "No, but I was thinking how much longer I can go on without Ruth." He then commented that he should not complain, "I have had a happy life."[4]

Ruth's death incited speculation that the senator would resign his office. Friend and supporter William Grant inquired, saying he had been asked "more than one hundred times" if Morrill would resign. Maine senator George F. Hoar wrote, citing a New York *Tribune* article speculating on Morrill's resignation and asked if it were true. Morrill consistently denied he would even think of resigning, "unless the infirmities of age should suddenly increase." Such talk "was simply gossip that somehow found its way into the newspaper." There were also questions of his intention to run for a seventh term in 1902, but he felt it was too early to decide about future elections.[5]

Morrill resumed his seat and his busy schedule when Congress met in December 1898. Later that month he caught a cold, but continued his daily trips to the Senate. Influenza followed the cold, but doctors did not believe it to be serious. Then pneumonia developed. He lapsed into a coma and died on 28 December 1898, with Louise and James at his bedside. Pres. William McKinley ordered all executive departments closed on 31 December in commemoration of his death. The body laid in state in the Senate chambers. At the memorial service, his friend Senator Hoar described him as "incorruptible" and lamented his loss to the nation. A funeral followed at the Washington All Souls' Church. There would be another later in Strafford.[6]

People across the nation mourned his passing, especially those in his native state. Flags over the capitol in Montpelier and other public buildings around the state flew at half-staff. The Central Vermont Railroad ran special trains so people could attend the funeral. Black borders adorned most newspapers. Citizens knew they had lost a remarkable public servant. Morrill had served in Congress continuously since December 1855, longer than anyone before him. During his tenure the nation had grown from fewer than 30 million to more than 70 million people. The federal budget increased from $66 million to nearly $690 million. Throughout that time, every bill he wrote and every tariff that passed through Congress reflected Vermont's interests, as well as those of the nation.[7]

After Justin's death, James and Louise believed he should have a final resting place befitting a man of his contributions and stature. His mausoleum, costing $10,000 in 1899, is of granite, marble, and steel. The eighteen by ten foot capstone of Barre, Vermont, granite weighs twenty-two tons. After the stone arrived in Sharon by train, workers winched it along the last twelve miles to Strafford using a windlass powered by twenty-four horses. A snowstorm interrupted the effort and workers had to wait until the spring to finish the task. The mausoleum was complete about 1 August 1899. The family, including Morrill's surviving sister and brothers, then gathered for Justin and Ruth's final interment. Today, the imposing structure looks quite out of place in the little cemetery overlooking Strafford. It is also the final resting place for James and Louise.[8]

Morrill's will, rewritten just two months before his death, left the bulk of his estate to James. Louise received iron and steel and bank stock and a store and two houses in Washington. The will also provided that if James died before Louise, the property left to him was to pass on to her. Morrill left his father's home to his nephew Henry. Morrill's estate paid Sister Edna and brother Wilbur $2,000 a year and established a $1,000 scholarship at the University of Vermont for a Strafford student "either male or female."[9]

James and Louise continued to share both the Washington and the Strafford homes. Elderly neighbors recalled James as short and stocky, with a "very impressive" moustache. He always dressed very well and drove a handsome carriage pulled by two beautiful Morgan horses. Local residents recounted James' visits to Strafford when he and his friend Charles Downer would race through town in their buggy, "visiting with everyone, including the French settlement." During winter visits, when Morrill's Strafford house was closed, the two would stay at Silloway's hotel and spend the night drinking. The next morning they would tap on the floor and Earl, the hotel owner's son, would take up a pitcher of water to quench their thirst. James apparently courted several local women, including Minnie Shoemaker, but neither he nor Louise ever married.[10]

On 26 July 1910, just twelve years after the death of his parents, James died. His real property, valued at an estimated $100,000, went to Louise for the duration of her life, then was to be divided among various cousins. The Strafford house would pass to Elmer E. Morrill and the farm to John Darling, an old employee. In addition, the University of Vermont received $20,000, to use as the trustees saw fit, $5,000 went to the Strafford cemetery to maintain the grounds and the Morrill mausoleum. The town inherited $3,000 for public roads and $1,000 for the library.[11]

James's death fell as a heavy blow on Louise. Her notes acknowledging sympathy cards spoke of the "great affliction" upon the death of her "beloved nephew." After a two-year period, during which her letters carried the black border of mourning, she resumed her role as the gracious host in the Washington house during the winter. Then come spring, the grand dame with her retinue of household help arrived in Strafford for the summer. Louise maintained a friendship with Charles Downer, who also served as her attorney. He showered her with flowers and candy and she loved the attention. She continued in her role until 18 November 1919, when she too died. As mentioned above, she shares the mausoleum with her sister's family.[12]

Although Justin Morrill left no descendants after the death of James, he left a lasting legacy. Anyone who has visited Washington and admired the beauty of the Library of Congress or the symmetry of the Capitol and its grounds can appreciate Morrill's efforts. His greatest contribution, however, was the Land-Grant College Act and the subsequent measures to strengthen and expand it. Millions of students, American industry, the military services, and the country in general have benefited. If Justin Morrill had done nothing else, the Land-Grant College Act would have assured his place in history.

Notes

1. Boston Transcript, 31 December 1898, LOC.
2. Morrill to Benedict, 14 July 1897, LOC.
3. Benedict to Morrill, 16 July 1897, LOC.
4. Louise Swan to Kate Sanborn, 29 December 1904, LOC.
5. Grant to Morrill, 15 September, 1 October 1898; Morrill to Grant, 16 September, 4 October 1898; Hoar to Morrill, 26 and 30 September 1898; Morrill to Kittridge Haskins, 29 September 1898, LOC.

6. "Justin Smith Morrill," *Vermonter,* January 1899; *Washington Evening Star,* 28 December 1898, LOC.
7. *New York Evening Post,* 30 December 1898; *Burlington Free Press and Times,* n.d., LOC.
8. *Bellows Falls Times,* 4 January 1899; New Albany, Indiana *Courier-Journal,* 6 August 1899, LOC.
9. The will of the late Senator Morrill, dated 28 October 1898, LOC.
10. Interview, Olive Lewis with Earl H. Silloway, 5 October 1979; notes from Rosa Tyson, Morrill House, Strafford, Vermont.
11. *Burlington Daily Free Press,* 2 February 1914, LOC.
12. Series of letters from Louise to Downer from 22 March 1909 to 22 June 1913; Jesse Morrill to Downer, 5 May 1911 and 6 February 1912, letters in possession of Sarah Donohue, Sharon, Vermont.

BIBLIOGRAPHY

Primary Sources

Unpublished

Morrill, Justin S., correspondence, Justin S. Morrill Collection, Chicago Historical Society.

———, correspondence and speeches, Justin S. Morrill Collection, Carl A. Kroch Library, Cornell University.

———, articles, Justin S. Morrill Collection, Baker Library, Dartmouth College.

———, correspondence, Justin S. Morrill Collection, Duke University Library.

———, correspondence, Justin S. Morrill Collection, Harvard University Library.

———, correspondence and speeches, Justin S. Morrill Collection, Library of Congress.

———, correspondence, Strafford Historical Society.

———, correspondence, Justin S. Morrill Collection, Syracuse University Library.

———, pictures, Justin S. Morrill Collection, Vermont Office of Historic Preservation.

———, correspondence and pictures, Justin S. Morrill Collection, Vermont Historical Society.

————, correspondence, Justin S. Morrill Collection, University of Vermont Library.

Morrill, Ruth S., correspondence, Swan Collection, Massachusetts Historical Society.

Swan, Louise, correspondence, private collection, Sarah Donohue.

Published

Adams, Charles Francis. *Charles Francis Adams, 1835–1915, An Autobiography.* Boston: Houghton Mifflin Company, 1916.

Blaine, James G. *Twenty Years in Congress.* Norwich Conn.: Henry Bill Company, 1884.

Boutwell, George S. *Reminiscences of Sixty Years in Public Affairs.* New York: McClure, Phillips and Co. 1902.

Chase, Salmon P. *Inside Lincoln's Cabinet, the Civil War Diaries of Salmon P. Chase.* Edited by David Donald. New York: Longmans, Green and Co., 1954.

————. "Diary and Correspondence of Salmon P. Chase" In *Annual Report of the American Historical Association for the Year 1902,* vol 2. Washington: Government Printing Office, 1903.

Hale, Edward Everett. *Memories of a Hundred Years.* New York: MacMillan Company, 1904.

Hayes, Rutherford B. *Hayes, The Diary of a President: 1875–1881.* Edited by T. Harry Williams. New York: David McKay Company, Inc., 1964.

Hoar, George F. *Autobiography of Seventy Years.* New York: Charles Scribner's Sons, 1903.

McCulloch, Hugh. *Men and Measures of Half a Century.* New York: Charles Scribner's Sons, 1900.

McKinley, William. *The Tariff: a review of the tariff legislation of the United States from 1812 to 1896.* New York: Putnam, 1904.

Morrill, Justin S. *Self-Consciousness of Noted Persons.* Boston: Ticknor and Company, 1887.

Sherman, John. *Recollections of Forty Years in the House, Senate and Cabinet.* Chicago: Werner Company, 1895.

Spaulding, E. G. *History of the Legal Tender Paper Money Issued During the Great Rebellion being a Loan without Interest and a National Currency.* Buffalo: Express Printing Co., 1869.

Secondary Sources

Published

After 100 Years: A Report by the State of Vermont Morrill Land-Grant Centennial Committee. Montpelier: 1962.

Allen, Herman R. *Open Door to Learning: The Land-Grant System Enters Its Second Century*. Urbana: University of Illinois Press, 1963.

Andreano, Ralph. *The Economic Impact of the American Civil War*. Cambridge: Schenkman Publishing Co., 1962.

Bartlett, Irving H. *Daniel Webster*. New York: W. W. Norton and Co, Inc., 1978.

Beale, Lucrece. *People to People: The Role of State and Land-Grant Universities in Modern America*. Washington: National Association of State Universities and Land-Grant Colleges, ca. 1979.

Benedict, Michael L. *The Impeachment and Trial of Andrew Johnson*. New York: W. W. Norton and Co., Inc., 1973.

Blue, Frederick J. *Salmon P. Chase, A Life in Politics*. Kent, Ohio: Kent State University Press, 1987.

Bolles, Albert S. *The Financial History of the United States From 1789 to 1860*. New York: Augustus M. Kelley Publishers, 1969.

Brodie, Fawn M. *Thaddeus Stevens, Scourge of the South*. New York: W. W. Norton and Company, Inc., 1959.

Christy, Ralph D. and Lionel Williamson, eds. *A Century of Service: land-grant colleges and universities, 1890–1990*. New Brunswick: Transaction Publishers, 1992.

Crook, D. P. *The North, the South, and the Powers, 1861–1865*. New York: John Wiley and Sons, 1974.

Davison, Kenneth E. *The Presidency of Rutherford B. Hayes*. Westport, Conn.: Greenwood Press, Inc., 1972.

Dewey, Davis Rich. *Financial History of the United States*. New York: Augustus M. Kelley Publishers, 1968.

Donald, David H. *Charles Sumner and the Rights of Man*. New York: Alfred A. Knopf, 1970.

———. *Lincoln*. New York: Simon and Schuster, 1995.

———. *The Politics of Reconstruction: 1863–67*. Cambridge: Harvard University Press, 1984.

Doyle, William. *The Vermont Political Tradition: And Those Who Helped Make It*. Barre Vt.: Northlight Studio Press, 1984.

Eddy, Edward D. Jr. *Colleges for Our Land and Time: The Land-Grant Idea in American Education.* New York: Harper and Brothers, 1956.

Edmond, J. B. *The Magnificent Charter: The Origin and Role of the Morrill Land-Grant Colleges and Universities.* Hicksville N.Y.: Exposition Press, 1978.

Fall 1993 Enrollment at Public, Four-Year Institutions. Washington: National Association of State Universities and Land-Grant Colleges, 1994.

Fessenden, Francis. *Life and Public Services of William Pitt Fessenden.* Boston: Houghton, Mifflin and Company, 1907.

Flint, Harrison L. "Some Horticultural Activities of Justin Smith Morrill." *Arnoldia,* 28 (7 June 1968).

Foner, Eric. *Reconstruction: America's Unfinished Revolution, 1863–1877.* New York: Harper and Row, Publishers, 1988.

Gates, Paul W. "Western Opposition to the Agricultural College Act." *Indiana Magazine of History,* 37 (March 1941).

Goldstein, Judith. *Ideas, Interests, and American Trade Policy.* Ithaca, N.Y.: Cornell University Press, 1993.

Hammond, Bray. *Sovereignty and an Empty Purse: Banks and Politics in the Civil War.* Princeton: Princeton University Press, 1970.

Haynes, Frederick E. *The Reciprocity Treaty with Canada of 1854.* Baltimore: American Economic Association, 1892.

Hoogenboom, Ari, and Olive Hoogenboom, eds. *The Gilded Age.* Englewood Cliffs, N.J.: Prentice-Hall, Inc. 1967.

Howe, Frederic C. *Taxation and Taxes in the United States under the Internal Revenue System, 1791–1895.* Boston: Thomas Y. Crowell and Company, 1896.

Ilisevich, Robert D. *Galusha A. Grow: The People's Candidate.* Pittsburgh: University of Pittsburgh Press, 1988.

Jacob, Kathryn A. *Capital Elites: High Society in Washington D.C. after the Civil War.* Washington: Smithsonian Institution Press, 1995.

James, Edmund J. *The Origin of the Land Grant Act of 1862 (The so-called Morrill Act) and Some Account of its Author Jonathan B. Turner.* Urbana: University of Illinois, 1910.

Jones, Howard. *The Union in Peril: The Crisis over British Intervention in the Civil War.* Chapel Hill: University of North Carolina Press, 1992.

Justin Smith Morrill, Centenary Exercises Celebrated by the state of Vermont at Montpelier April Fourteenth Nineteen Hundred and Ten. Fulton, NY: Morrill Press, 1910.

Larson, Henrietta M. *Jay Cooke, Private Banker.* Cambridge: Harvard University Press, 1936.

Lessoff, Alan, *The Nation and Its City: Politics, "Corruption," and Progress in Washington, D.C. 1861–1902.* Baltimore: Johns Hopkins Press, 1994.

McCall, Samuel W. *Thaddeus Stevens.* Boston: Houghton, Mifflin and Company, 1899.

Middleton, Allen H. Arthur A. Attwell, and Gregory O. Walsh. *Epilepsy.* Boston: Little Brown and Company, 1981.

Milton, George F. *The Age of Hate: Andrew Johnson and the Radicals.* New York: Coward-McCann, Inc. 1930.

Mitchell, Wesley Clair. *History of the Greenbacks.* Chicago: The University of Chicago Press, 1903.

Monaghan, Jay. *Diplomat in Carpet Slippers: Abraham Lincoln Deals with Foreign Affairs.* Indianapolis: Bobbs-Merrill Company, 1945.

Morgan, H. Wayne, ed. *The Gilded Age: A Reappraisal.* Syracuse: Syracuse University Press, 1963.

Morrissey, Charles T. *Vermont: A Bicentennial History.* New York: W. W. Norton and Company, Inc. 1981.

Nevins, Allan. *Ordeal of the Union: A House Dividing, 1852–1857.* New York: Charles Scribner's Sons, 1947.

———. *The Emergence of Lincoln.* New York: Charles Scribner's Sons, 1950.

———. *The Origins of the Land-Grant Colleges and State Universities.* Washington: Civil War Centennial Commission, 1962.

———. *The State Universities and Democracy.* Urbana: University of Illinois Press, 1962.

———. *War for the Union.* New York: Charles Scribner's Sons, 1959.

Nichols, Roy F. *The Stakes of Power, 1845–1877.* New York: Hill and Wang, 1961.

Parker, William Belmont. *The Life and Public Services of Justin Smith Morrill.* Boston: Houghton Mifflin Company, 1924.

Potter, David M. *Lincoln and His Party in the Secession Crisis.* New Haven: Yale University Press, 1962.

Ratner, Sidney. *The Tariff in American History.* New York: D. Van Nostrand Company, 1972.

Rawley, James A. *The Politics of Union: Northern Politics during the Civil War*. Lincoln: University of Nebraska Press, 1974.

Reitano, Joanne. *The Tariff Question in the Gilded Age: The Great Debate of 1888*. University Park: Pennsylvania University Press, 1994.

Ross, Earle D. *Democracy's College: The Land-Grant Movement in the Formative Stage*. Ames: The Iowa State College Press, 1942.

Ross, Edmund G. *History of the Impeachment of Andrew Johnson*. New York: Burt Franklin, 1896.

Saum, Lewis O. *The Popular Mood of America, 1860–1890*. Lincoln: University of Nebraska Press, 1990.

Schuckers, J. W. *The Life and Public Services of Salmon Portland Chase, United States Senator and Governor of Ohio; Secretary of the Treasury, and Chief Justice of the United States*. New York: D. Appleton and Company, 1874.

Seligman, Edwin R. A. *The Income Tax: A study of the history, theory, and practice of income taxation at home and abroad*. New York: MacMillan Company, 1911.

Sharkey, Robert P. *Money, Class, and Party: An Economic Study of Civil War and Reconstruction*. Baltimore: The Johns Hopkins Press, 1959.

Silbey, Joel H. *The American Political Nation, 1838–1893*. Stanford: Stanford University Press, 1991.

Smith, Anne Morrill. *Morrill Kindred in America: An Account of the Descendants of Abraham Morrill of Salisbury Massachusetts, 1632–1662, Through His Eldest Son Isaac Morrill, 1640–1713*. New York: Lyons Genealogical Company, 1914.

Smith, Donnal V. *Chase and Civil War Politics*. Columbus: F. J. Heer Printing Co. 1931.

Socologsky, Homer E. and Allan B. Spetter. *The Presidency of Benjamin Harrison*. Lawrence, Kan.: University Press of Kansas, 1987.

Stampp, Kenneth M. *America in 1857: A Nation on the Brink*. New York: Oxford University Press, 1990.

———. *The Era of Reconstruction: 1865–1877*. New York: Vintage Books, 1967.

Stanley, Robert. *Dimensions of Law in the Service of Order: Origins of the Federal Income Tax, 1861–1913*. New York: Oxford University Press, 1993.

Stanwood, Edward. *American Tariff Controversies in the Nineteenth Century*. New York: Russell and Russell, 1904.

Summers, Mark W. *The Era of Good Stealings.* New York: Oxford University Press, 1993.

Taussig, F. W. *The History of the Present Tariff, 1860–1883.* New York: G. P. Putnam's Sons, 1888.

———. *The Tariff History of the United States.* New York: G. P. Putnam's Sons, 1931.

Thackrey, Russell I. *The Future of the State University.* Urbana: University of Illinois Press, 1971.

Thackrey, Russell I. and Jay Richter. "The Land-Grant Colleges and Universities, 1862–1962, An American Institution." *Higher Education* 16 (November 1959).

Trefousse, Hans L. *Impeachment of a President: Andrew Johnson, the Blacks, and Reconstruction.* Knoxville: University of Tennessee Press, 1975.

———. *The Radical Republicans: Lincoln's Vanguard for Racial Justice.* New York: Alfred A. Knopf, 1969.

Wahlquist, John T. and James W. Thornton, Jr. *State Colleges and Universities.* Washington: The Center for Applied Research in Education, Inc. 1964.

Welch, Richard E. Jr. *The Presidencies of Grover Cleveland.* Lawrence, Kan.: University Press of Kansas, 1988.

Williams, Roger L. *The Origins of Federal Support for Higher Education: George W. Atherton and the Land-Grant College Movement.* University Park PA: The Pennsylvania State University Press, 1991.

Wilson, Harold F. *The Hill Country of New England: Its Social and Economic History, 1790–1930.* New York: Columbia University Press, 1936.

Woodburn, James A. *The Life of Thaddeus Stevens.* Indianapolis: The Bobbs-Merrill Company, Publishers, 1913.

York, Barbara, "The Morrill Homestead." University of Vermont, 1983.

Unpublished:

Freeman, Yvonne. "The Formation of the Black Land-Grant Colleges." Morrill Homestead, 1992.

Hayes, Merwyn A. "The Andrew Johnson Impeachment Trial: A Case Study in Argumentation." Masters thesis, University of Illinois, 1966.

Hoyer, Randal L. "The Gentleman From Vermont: The Career of Justin S. Morrill in the United States House of Representatives." Ph.D. diss., Michigan State University, 1974.

Key, Scott A. "The Origins of American Land Grant Universities: An Historical Policy Study." Ph.D. diss., University of Illinois, Chicago, 1995.

Welch, Robert W., "Rhetorical Study of the Legislative Speaking of Congressman Justin Smith Morrill of Vermont in the U.S. House of Representatives on Selected Issues," *1855–1867*. Ph.D. diss., Pennsylvania State University, 1977.

Newspapers

Bellows Falls *Times*
Boston *Transcript*
Burlington *Free Press*
Montpelier *Free Press and Times*
Great Salt Lake City *Mountaineer*
New Albany *Courier-Journal*
New York *Evening Post*
Portland *Advocate*
Washington *Evening Star*
Washington Post

INDEX OF PROPER NAMES AND PLACES